DIAMOND LEADERSHIP

VIKTOR KUNOVSKI

Creating alignment and innovation in your system

catalyst@skyisthelimit.org

Viktor Kunovski © 2018

"DIAMOND LEADERSHIP"

"With power, must come wisdom"

A co-creative, presence-based leadership guide for creating alignment and liberating the creative and innovative potential in people, organizations and nations

For my daughter Mia and the generations to come

CONTENTS

INTRODUCTION

Why this book?
National leadership for the 21st century
A few facts about Macedonia
The beginning
How did we start?

VISUALIZATION

PART I

Values and culture
The model of the seven levels of consciousness
A detailed description of the model
Seven levels of consciousness on a personal level
A detailed description of the model on a national level (society/community)
Full spectrum of consciousness
Preparation for the measurement
Results of measurement: 1 – Big gap in values
Results of measurement: 2 - Low levels of alignment
Results of measurement: 3 - High entropy
Results of measurement: 4 - Strategy for growth not supported
Full Assessment
Back to corporation Macedonia
The example of Unilever Brazil
Culture eats strategy for breakfast, AGAIN!
A few words about the "good", and why it is the greatest enemy of the "GREAT"

PART II

Systemic leadership – "Co-Creation"
Collective intelligence
Systemic intelligence is always smarter and wiser than the leader or the leadership team
System leaders – "Co-Creators"
Creative dialogue
Creative dialogue is not the same as the dialogue we know
Modern methods and tools
What makes creative dialogue innovative and inspirational?
"U Theory", creative dialogue and corporation Macedonia
Key questions for creative dialogue
Bad dialogue is only the dialogue that we don't have
Slow down, to speed up
Collective illumination – breakthrough
Key questions for corporation Macedonia
Other key questions
Presence – "The key to conscious and authentic leadership"

INTRODUCTION

Why this book?

I write these words because I feel and see, all around us, the unfolding of the biggest change in consciousness and the most radical culture shift that humankind has ever witnessed - the paradigm shift from the "Ego to Eco" functioning of our organizations, communities and nations.

From global warming and drastic climate changes, to the financial instability in the markets, to the growing gap between the poor and rich, the facts and the data are more than obvious and they show that we are not producing the results that humanity and the planet require, in order to create well-being and ensure the survival of the generations to come. Instead, we are working against ourselves and against nature's logic and wisdom, and unnecessarily wasting much of our energies and resources.

So how, in these challenging times, are we to become a truly sustainable civilization? How can we align with nature's wisdom, and create innovative solutions and results that actually work for the benefit of the whole?
How can we design organizations that are more efficient, resilient and adaptable to change? How can we stop wasting energy, time and money, and become a truly balanced and sustainable society?

These are not simple questions, and this book does not intend to answer them all. In order to reach the answers, we need to approach things in a different and innovative way, which requires new ways of thinking and answering, new leadership models and skills. We require a new way of knowing that is not ego-based, but is rather a reflection of the collective intelligence of the whole wider system.

What the world will look like during and after these changes, I do not at present know. This is a matter of evolution itself. My assumption and wish is that people, organizations and nations on the planet will in the future function more wholly and with a greater alignment between our selves and with our nature. It is my hope that the examples and the experiences in this book will assist leaders and organizations during the challenging processes of this shift.

I originally wrote the book in my mother tongue – for the Macedonian public, because my projects and work at the time had taken me back there. As the writing progressed and I reflected on the experiences of leaders and companies around the world that had walked this path before us in Macedonia, I realized that this is not a book on Macedonia alone. The challenges Macedonia faces today are incredibly similar to the realities of many other organizations, regions and nations worldwide.

In the pages that follow I will approach Macedonia as a system, an organization, a business – not just as a country. This is because the principles of transformation and the solutions to challenges for companies and nations are in essence very similar.

Because of this similarity, I will often refer to Macedonia as **corporation Macedonia**, and I believe that the reader will very quickly recognize many similarities between his system and that of Macedonia.

The first part of this book focuses on the present state of Corporation Macedonia, and the diagnostic tool that we used to assess the culture and functioning of the system. Because of the paramount importance of this diagnostic assessment, the first part focuses on lightly but accurately describing the model behind the diagnostic tool – the Barrett seven levels of consciousness model.

The second part of the book is about shedding some light on the question of how we actually make this shift – not just in corporation Macedonia but in companies and systems all over the world. This part offers insights into the latest innovative models and tools that are currently being used, and are available to leaders and change agents who are spearheading or contributing to such activities around the world.

Despite the actual complexity of some models mentioned and described in this book, my primary intention is not to be heavily eloquent and academic about them; therefore, wherever possible, I have balanced simplicity with accuracy, and used plain words instead of complex jargon. All of this has been done for one reason, and that is to make this book accessible to anyone out there in our system who is interested in leading, contributing to, and co-creating, with small or big steps, the change that is so greatly needed in our communities, our organizations, and in the world.

National leadership for the 21ˢᵗ century

The initial purpose of this book, and the significance of the processes described in it, lies in the creation of a Macedonian society that will be characterized with exceptional values in our national culture/s, together with the innovative and creative performance of our citizens, institutions, and companies, at all levels – from sport and culture, to politics and business, to new models of global leadership.

These processes, when supported and implemented, could take Macedonia from the current dire socio-economic position, to having a world class leadership team; from being a mediocre economic performer, to becoming a lean speed boat.

The methodologies and tools that are mentioned, used and proposed in this book are currently applied globally, at both the individual and organizational level (companies, cities, and nations), regardless of the size of the organization.

A few facts about Macedonia

Full Name: The Republic of Macedonia, one of the successor states of the former Yugoslavia. Geographically, Macedonia is placed in South-East Europe in the heart of the Balkan Peninsula.

Area: 25,713 sq. km. (9,928 sq. miles)

Population: 2.06 million (UN, 2009)

Capital: Skopje, population 668,518

Ethnic Groups: Macedonians: 64.2%, Albanians: 25.2%, Turks: 3.9%, Roma: 2.7%, Serbs: 1.8%, others: 2.2%.

GDP: $10.055 billion (IMF, 2013)

The Macedonian Budget in 2014: 2,870,000,000 euros (Macedonian Ministry of Finances)

GDP Per Capita (Nominal): US $4,589 (World Bank, 2012). Macedonia ranks in the 83rd place in the world in this category.

Official Unemployment: Remains high at 28.6% (2013 Q4), but may be overstated based on the existence of an extensive gray market, which is estimated to be more than 20% of the GDP, but is not captured by official statistics (CIA).

Foreign Direct Investment (FDI): Has so far lagged in the region, despite extensive fiscal and business sector reforms (CIA). Despite the extensive governmental campaign and support for FDI, Macedonia is one of the poorest performers in this area in the Western Balkans and South-East Europe.

Average Salary in June 2010: 330 euro. This ranks Macedonians among the lowest earners in Europe.

Main Exports: Food processing, beverages, textiles, chemicals, iron and steel, cement, energy, pharmaceuticals.

The beginning

Macedonia is the first country in South-East Europe that has made an assessment (precise diagnosis) of its own values and its national culture.

This makes Macedonia one of the few countries in the world[1] that have embarked on such a process, and puts the country in the position of being a regional leader and equitable global player in this important transformational and evolutionary process.

The process of measuring and managing culture in an organizational context is named organizational **culture transformation**. The same process on a national level can be named **national culture transformation**. Therefore the measurement made in 2009 began the unstoppable process of national culture transformation in Macedonia.

How did we start?

The values assessment was ordered by the client USAID Macedonia, and delivered by the consultancy COACH ERA, together with the world leader in this field, the Barrett Values Centre.

In April 2009, the assessment began by measuring the values and culture of citizens in the Skopje region. This region has 18 municipalities and includes over 550,000 people from urban and suburban communities around the capital. Given that Skopje has almost a third of the total population of Macedonia and is a smaller version of the country, this regional measurement can be considered to also be a national one.

For the assessment, we used one of the tools from the palette of Culture Transformation Tools (CTT). These tools were designed in the last decade of the 20th century by Richard Barrett, and represent a cutting-edge technology in the process of measuring and managing leadership values and organizational culture. The CTT were originally designed

---

[1] As of June 2014, 26 countries have have performed national culture assessments:
http://www.valuescentre.com/uploads/2014-05-21/National%20Values%20Resource%20Guide%20June%202014%20v5.pdf

to be used in the business context, primarily to help leaders to align their organizational strategy and culture with the values of the executive leadership team.

In the past decade, since they have proved to be excellent for this purpose and have been used by over 6,000 companies in 90 countries worldwide, the CTT have begun to be used on a regional and national level, to measure national cultures as well as help the processes of national culture transformation. Australia, Belgium, Bhutan, Brazil, Canada, Denmark, Finland, France, Hungry, Iceland, Latvia, Nigeria, Singapore, Slovakia, South Africa, Sweden, Switzerland, Trinidad and Tobago, Turkey, United Arab Emirates, UK, USA, and Venezuela have all undertaken a national cultural measurement (some of them repeatedly).

VISUALIZATION
INSPIRATION

I have decided to offer this visualization at the beginning of the book since I feel it is appropriate for the co-creational processes described inside. You can do this exercise alone, or in a group. In the second case, it would be ideal if someone guides you through the visualization.

Find a quiet place, sit in a chair without leaning on it and straighten your spine. Put your hands on your knees or upper legs. Spend few moments in stillness, relaxed and in peace, become present. Start sensing the fingers of your hands and feet, than slowly spread your sensing all over your body. Become aware of the totality of your body.
If your focus runs away, slowly and without judging yourself come back to your sensing. Maintain your intention to stay **present**.

Imagine and visualize in your mind's eye, at the height of your forehead, a glowing transparent diamond. Notice its clarity, transparency, purity and shine. Pay attention to its sharp edges, precise angles, and the breakings of the light inside.

Listen to the sound and the gentle vibration that come from the diamond. The diamond is the finest form of crystal that has a specific, almost vibrating, low-frequency sound.
Feel the feelings that come as you are in contact with the diamond.

Then slowly start to increase the size of the diamond, and bring it even closer to you. Make it bigger than yourself, and when it's sufficiently large, slowly enter inside of it.

Observe the light, purity and the clarity of the diamond, now from the inside. Hear the sound of the vibration from this place. Feel the vibration as well, and feel your body being affected by this new perspective of being within the diamond. Take several slow and deep breaths.
At the same time see, hear and sense the world from this place.

Notice again the hundreds of angles and corners of the diamond.
Imagine how hundreds of people are starting to approach the diamond. Your friends are among them, colleagues, fellow citizens and people from all over the world, all slowly coming towards you, and entering the diamond in silence. Only the gentle vibration is present.
The diamond is growing and it has a place to hold all the people. You can see their eyes perfectly clear and bright. Your heart is warming and expanding.

In the distance on the horizon the sun appears, its rays of light touch the diamond and all the people in it. The light gently breaks, and illuminates all corners and reaches all the people inside the diamond. The glow is growing stronger, and through the sharp corners of the diamond, begins to radiate luminous, brilliantly shining, powerful beams of light with pure energy, that touch every village, town, state, country, and the entire planet. The light beam radiates and spreads across the galaxy and through the universe.

Gently remind yourself of your body, feel your fingers, arms and legs. Slowly, in your own time, open your eyes, and stay present in your chair.
You may share your experience with others in the group.

PART I
THE MEASUREMENT

Identical to organizational culture, national culture is the sum of the values and behaviors of the people within the system.

Values and culture

Who you are and what you stand for is just as important as what you do.

When an unknown traveler meets you somewhere in the world and wonders who you are and where you come from, the first initial response would be that you come from and are Macedonian. If the traveler is a curious one (which is usually the case), the conversation would slowly spread to the kind of food and customs we have as a people, the climate, and eventually the economic situation, the political system of the country, the infrastructure, etc. Of course this exchange would most often be mutual, so you would also learn more about the origins of your new friend.

Sometimes these initial meetings develop into new contacts and friendships, and often our friends are invited for a closer meeting in our homes, where we get to know them further. Here we offer our beautiful salad, white cheese, home-made pastries and a glass of wonderful Macedonia wine. Here we exchange the first "cheers" or "to health", as Macedonians say when we drink with friends...

All of these behaviors are expressions that manifest our values (such as hospitality, friendship, creativity, etc.); and these values make up our character as individuals.

On a personal level, values create our character and are manifested through it.

When, after the meal at home, we take our new friends to show them around the neighborhood, our town, or the country, we present them with the wider range of values and behaviors that are part of our characters as well as part of the **culture** of our bigger family – our people and nation.

On the collective level, the values and behaviors of people in the system create the culture of the system.

In this context, our values are the bricks that build the house of our nation, and the culture of the nation as a whole is shaped by the values and attitudes of people who build the house.

In brief, the values and culture are the identity card or DNA of a nation.

The model of the seven levels of consciousness

In order to fully understand the process of measuring and transforming the culture of any organization, whether in corporation Macedonia or any other nation, at the beginning it is necessary to describe the model of the seven levels of consciousness. This step is important since the model takes a central place in the structure of the Culture Transformation Tools (CTT).

The model of the seven levels of consciousness has been created by Richard Barrett and is fully explained in his book "Building a Values-Driven Organization"[2]. This is an upgrade of the well-known Maslow model of the hierarchy of human needs, wherein Barrett has adapted and enriched Maslow's model by adding some old Eastern Vedic wisdom.

---

[2] "Building a Values-Driven Organization" Richard Barrett, Butterworth-Heinemann 2006

Richards latest book on this subject is "The Values-Driven Organization" - Unleashing Human Potential for Performance and Profit, Routledge 2013

The Model of the 7 levels of consciousness
From Maslow to Barrett

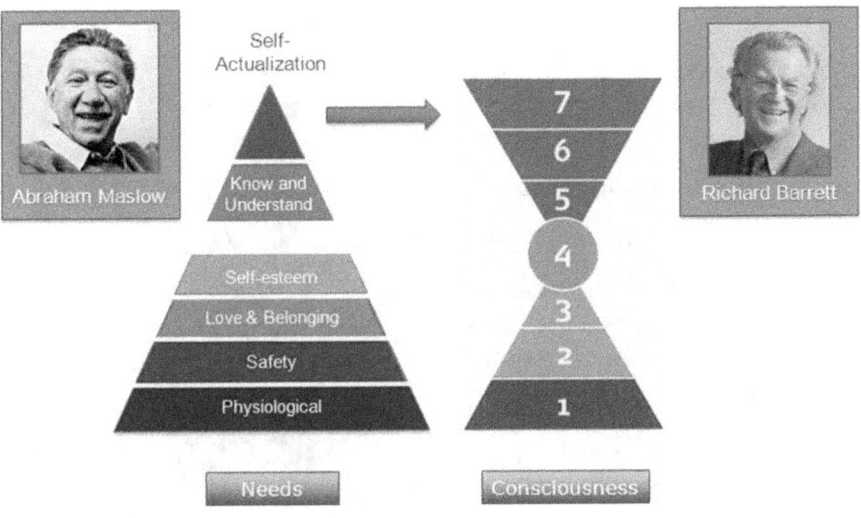

Picture 1.1: The model of the seven levels of consciousness: From Maslow to Barrett

What are defined as needs in Maslow's model, become levels of consciousness in Barrett's model.

Barrett merges the physiological and safety needs in the first level of consciousness, which he calls **Survival**. The needs for love and belonging represent the second level of consciousness, called **Relationships**. The need for self-esteem becomes level three of consciousness, named **Self-Esteem**. Mental needs become the fourth level of consciousness, termed **Transformation**. Barrett expands the spiritual needs described by Maslow into three separate levels of consciousness. Level five is called **Internal Cohesion**, level six is **Making a Difference** and level seven is termed **Service**.

The model of the seven levels of consciousness is applicable to all people at the individual level, as well as to all organizations, communities and nations, without exception.

7 levels of consciousness

Human needs	Human Motivation	
Spiritual	Service	7
	Making a difference	6
	Internal cohesion	5
Mental	Transformation	4
Emotional	Self-esteem	3
	Relationships	2
Physical	Survival	1

Picture 1.2: Barrett's seven levels of consciousness

To date, this model has been used by over 6,000 organizations and companies in the world, including governmental and non-governmental organizations, and educational institutions.

In order to really simplify this model and make it accessible to every reader, I use the analogy of a car that has a seven-cylinder engine. All individuals and/or organizations have seven available levels – cylinders with which they can operate.
Each level of cylinder has a specific function and produces a certain energy, which is represented by the particular values that belong to that level. In everyday life, these values manifest through our actions and behaviors. The values and behaviors can be positive (profit, vision, leadership, creativity, excellence...) or limiting (environmental pollution, corruption, arrogance, fear, etc.).

The limiting values appear as a result of our unconscious fears, and the belief that our needs will not be met and that our survival will be threatened and challenged. They only exist at the first three levels of consciousness in Barrett's model.

The fears at the first level (Survival) are about not being safe and secure, and not having enough for "me" (at a personal level) or for "us" (at the organizational/systemic level). As a reaction to this unconscious motivation, limiting behaviors such as crime, violence, corruption, and a short-term focus appear, among others.

The second-level fears (Relationships) are about not being valued or loved, and not belonging to the community. The unconscious motivation at this level can be seen in the limiting values and behaviors of blaming, discrimination, manipulation, etc.

The fears at the third level (Self-Esteem) are about not being good enough. The limiting behaviors triggered by these fears are bureaucracy, illiteracy, self-interest, etc.

If any level is dominated (blocked) by the limiting values, it does not work properly, and the energy of the leader (if observed individually) or that of the organization remains low, without the full utilization of the potential of that energy level. As a result, the creativity, productivity and efficiency that normally come from this level are reduced.

It is particularly important to emphasize that if there is a blockage at a particular level in the consciousness of the leader or the executive leadership team, the leaders' functioning with limiting values will be directly reflected in the functioning of the organization. As Richard puts it:

The organizational culture is a reflection of the leadership values.

In this context, limiting values are like cancer cells in the human body, and if the leadership structures are ailing with them, the whole system is threatened and in danger.

According to this model, all human group structures grow and develop in seven well-defined stages. Each stage focuses on a particular level of consciousness. These seven existential needs are the main motivation and driving force for all human and/or organizational activities.

The level of growth and development of the organization depends on the ability of leaders to create conditions that allow members to meet these seven

existential needs. If their needs are not met, then the consciousness of people in the group structure will remain focused on these needs, until their satisfaction.

A detailed description of the model

The model of the seven levels of consciousness is used to enhance the leaders' knowledge and their leadership skills and styles. It is also used to help companies, communities and nations to create well-aligned and innovative cultures.
There are several applications and descriptions of the model[3] (personal, leadership, team, organizational, national, etc.) I will stick to the two descriptions that are most relevant in the context of this book. These are the descriptions at the personal and the national level.

Seven levels of consciousness on a personal level

Level 1: Survival

Level 1 focuses on the physiological and survival needs of an individual. It includes values such as financial stability, health, nutrition and self-discipline.
The potentially limiting aspects of this level are generated from fears of not having enough, and not being able to survive. Limiting values include greed, control and caution.

Level 2: Relationships

Level 2 focuses on the quality of interpersonal relationships in the lives of individuals. It includes values such as open communication, family, friendship, conflict resolution and respect.

---

[3] http://www.valuescentre.com/culture/?sec=barrett_model

Potentially limiting aspects of this level are generated by the fears of not belonging, not being acknowledged or loved enough. Limiting values at this level include jealousy, rivalry, intolerance, and a dislike of others.

Level 3: Self-Esteem

Level 3 focuses on an individual's need to feel a sense of personal value. This includes values such as: excellence, competence, career focus, and a sense of reward. Potentially limiting aspects of this level are generated by the fear of not being good enough in the eyes of others, and a lack of positive self-worth. The limiting values include status consciousness, arrogance, and preoccupation with one's personal image.

Note: The first three levels of consciousness are also called levels of **self-interest**, mostly affected by our **ego** and/or **super-ego activities**. The levels 5, 6 and 7 are called **common good**, and could be called **"ECO"**[4] **or soul consciousness. There are no potentially limiting values in levels 4 to 7.**

Level 4: Transformation

Level 4 focuses on self-actualization and personal growth. It contains values such as courage, accountability, responsibility, knowledge and independence.
At this level individuals overcome the anxiety and fears that originate from the first three levels of consciousness. This is also the level where individuals begin to find a balance in their lives, and decisions are made on the basis of their values, not on the basis of their beliefs.

---

[4] In the current literature on leadership, the term from **"ego to eco leaders"** is used more and more often. See the works of Edgar H. Schein and Otto Scharmer in the second part of this book.

Level 5: Internal Cohesion

Level 5 focuses on the individual's search for meaning. Individuals operating at this level no longer think separately in terms of job or career; rather, they think of how to merge and connect their work with their personal mission, passion and purpose.
This level contains values such as dedication, creativity, enthusiasm, humor/fun, purpose and honesty.

Level 6: Making a difference

Level 6 focuses on the actualization of the sense of mission of the individual, thereby making a positive difference in the world. Individuals operating at this level seek to cultivate their intuition as their principal means of making decisions. They also recognize the importance of working with others to leverage their influence in the world.
This level contains values such as empathy, counseling, community work and environmental awareness.

Level 7: Serving

Level 7 is attained when making changes becomes a way of life. This reflects the highest order of internal and external connection, and is displayed as selfless service to others or to a particular cause.
Individuals operating at this level display wisdom, compassion, and forgiveness; they are at ease with the unknown and with uncertainty. They have a global perspective. They are concerned about issues such as social justice, human rights and future generations.

A detailed description of the model on the national level (society/community)

Level 1: Survival

The three main areas of focus or concern in communities that operate from this level of consciousness are safety, the economic prosperity of the masses, and the health and nutrition of all of its citizens.
Dysfunction on this level leads to unemployment, corruption, environmental degradation and large income disparities between the rich and poor, which in turn is the source of crime and violence, because groups whose survival is endangered tend to fulfill their needs in every possible way.

Level 2: Relationships

At this level of consciousness, the focus is on the peaceful resolution of conflict between individuals and groups, creating a sense of belonging that includes all the citizens in the system, thus creating a loyalty among citizens towards the government of that community/nation.
Dysfunction in this area leads to inter-ethnic or inter-religious violence, and the victimization or unfair treatment of minorities or sub-groups based on gender, sexual orientation and race, thus creating isolation and hatred.

Level 3: Self-Esteem

The areas of focus in communities that operate from this level of consciousness are: the introduction and enforcement of law and order, the creation of institutions of governance based on efficient systems and processes, and the provision of public infrastructure and services that enhance the productivity and well-being of the community and the prosperity of the people.
Dysfunction in this area leads to problems in accessing public services, a higher incidence of crime, and a lack of public protection from unscrupulous businesses.

Note: **There are no potentially limiting values in levels 4 to 7.**

Level 4: Transformation

The focus of the fourth level of national consciousness is the consolidation of internal stability, by creating a multicultural, egalitarian society that respects the rights of all citizens. This is a level of freedom and democracy, where citizens act responsibly for the good of all, with a focus on continuous improvement and renewal.

Level 5: Internal Cohesion

At this level the focus is on deepening the internal resilience of the community, by focusing on fairness, openness and transparency, and thereby creating an atmosphere of trust. At this level there is a sense of shared vision and values (collective spirit) where citizens have a role to play in building the community.

Level 6: Making a difference

The sixth level of consciousness focuses on developing strategic alliances and partnerships with neighboring nations, for mutually beneficial outcomes. There is a willingness to relinquish certain aspects of sovereignty to regional alliances. There is also a focus on the quality of life, environmental awareness, and animal welfare.

Level 7: Service

The seventh level focuses on expanding international cooperation, and working with other nations to build regional and global alliances that support solving the challenges and problems of humanity and the planet. The focus in societies operating at this level is on human rights, social justice, the welfare of future generations, the global environment, and the Earth's ecology. There is a recognition of the interconnectedness of all life.

Values and behaviors at the seven levels

For further clarity and orientation, the next seven slides will illustrate the model, outlining some of the key values and behaviors for each level of consciousness. There are values present at the personal, organizational and national level.

The limiting values are in **italic letters.** They appear only for the first three levels.

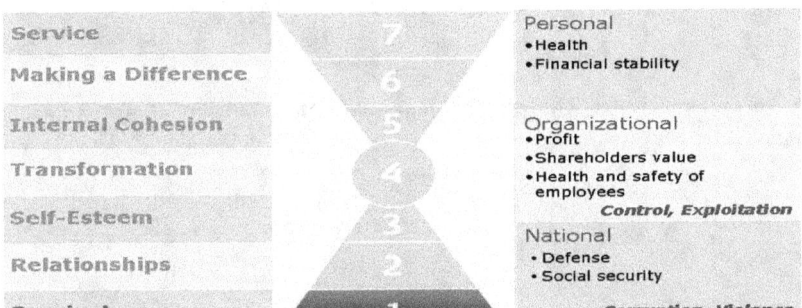

Survival

Primary focus: Base for survival

Service	Personal
	• Health
Making a Difference	• Financial stability
Internal Cohesion	
	Organizational
Transformation	• Profit
	• Shareholders value
Self-Esteem	• Health and safety of employees
	Control, Exploitation
Relationships	National
	• Defense
Survival	• Social security
	Corruption, Violence, Poverty, Greed, Pollution

Picture 1.3: Personal, organizational and national values and behaviors at level 1 – Survival

Relationships

Primary focus: Relationships and connectivity

Level		
Service	7	Personal • Family • Friendship
Making a Difference	6	
Internal Cohesion	5	Organizational • Customer satisfaction • Open communication • Respect *Blame, Manipulation*
Transformation	4	
Self-Esteem	3	National • Conflict resolution • Racial – Ethnic harmony • Rituals *Inequality, discrimination, intolerance, conflict-aggression.*
Relationships	2	
Survival	1	

Picture 1.4: Personal, organizational and national values and behaviors at level 2 – Relationships

Self Esteem

Primary focus: Self-esteem & excellence

Level		
Service	7	Personal • Self-confidence • Success
Making a Difference	6	
Internal Cohesion	5	Organizational • Efficiency • Productivity • Quality *Bureaucracy, wasted resources*
Transformation	4	
Self-Esteem	3	National • Law enforcement • Effective government *Centralized control, elitism, illiteracy*
Relationships	2	
Survival	1	

Picture 1.5: Personal, organizational and national values and behaviors at level 3 – Self-Esteem

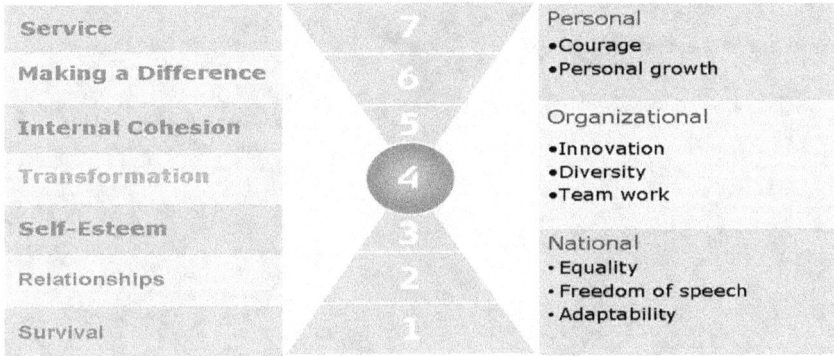

Picture 1.6: Personal, organizational and national values and behaviors at level 4 – Transformation

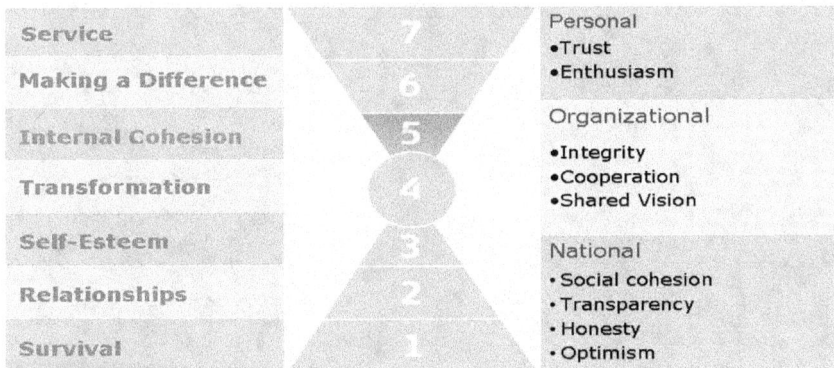

Picture 1.7: Personal, organizational and national values and behaviors at level 5 – Internal Cohesion

Making a Difference

Primary focus: Collaboration

Level		
Service	7	Personal • Mentoring • Volunteer work
Making a Difference	6	
Internal Cohesion	5	Organizational • Employee fulfillment • Environmental awareness • Strategic alliances
Transformation	4	
Self-Esteem	3	National • Quality of life • Leadership • Regional collaboration
Relationships	2	
Survival	1	

Picture 1.8: Personal, organizational and national values and behaviors at level 6 – Making a Difference

Service

Примарен Фокус: Служење на останатите

Level		
Service	7	Personal • Wisdom • Humility
Making a Difference	6	
Internal Cohesion	5	Organisational • Ethics • Future generations • Long-Term Perspective
Transformation	4	
Self-Esteem	3	National • Human rights • Peace • Ecological awareness
Relationships	2	
Survival	1	

Picture 1.9: Personal, organizational and national values and behaviors at level 7 – Service

Full spectrum of consciousness

What is extremely important to note when talking about the model of the seven levels of consciousness is that no level is better, or more important, than any other level.
What we need to achieve is to operate holistically (as a whole), on the entire spectrum – to attain a **full spectrum of consciousness** or simply speaking, personally and organizationally, to drive on all seven cylinders.

What is needed now are leaders who can help us bring our wholeness – our physical, intellectual, emotional, social and purposeful selves – to work on a daily basis.

Nick Udal

Preparation for the measurement

199 Macedonian citizens were each given three lists of values. Every citizen had to choose only 10 values from each list, in order to answer the following three questions:

1) Which 10 values best describe who you are (not who you want to be)?
2) Which 10 values best describe the current functioning of your municipality-town?
3) Which 10 values would you most like to see in your municipality-town?

The list of values for the first question contained 87 values. The lists for the second and the third question had 100 values each, all of which are given below.

Accountability	Fairness	Self-reliance
Adaptability	Family	Sense of community
Affordable housing	Financial stability	Shared values
Blame	Forgiveness	Shared vision
Bureaucracy	Freedom of speech	Short-term focus
Caring for the disadvantaged	Gender discrimination	Social cohesion
Caring for the elderly	Global thinking	Social justice
Centralized government	Governmental effectiveness	Social responsibility
Collaboration	Hatred	Solidarity
Commitment	Helpfulness	Spirituality
Community pride	Honesty	Strategic alliances
Community services	Human rights	Strict moral/religious codes
Compassion	Humility	Sustainability
Concern for future generations	Illiteracy	Terrorism
Conflict resolution	Innovation	Tolerance
Conflict/aggression	Integrity	Tradition
Corruption	Interdependence	Transparency
Creativity	Law enforcement	Trust
Crime/violence	Leadership	Uncertainty about future
Decentralization	Legal rights	Unemployment
Democratic process	Long-term perspective	Values awareness
Dependable public services	Making a difference	Wasted resources
Diversity	Material needs	Wisdom
Ecological awareness	Materialistic	Nepotism
Educational opportunities	Optimism	Economic growth
Effective healthcare	Peace	Inclusiveness
Elitism	Personal freedom	Environmental protection
Employment opportunities	Personal fulfillment	Isolation
Entrepreneurial	Poverty	Proactivity
Environmental awareness	Poverty reduction	Pessimism
Environmental pollution	Prosperity	Community partnerships
Equality	Quality of life	Community engagement
Ethics	Respect	Voluntary work
Ethnic discrimination		

Furthermore, the group of citizens was measured in ideal demographic balance. Measurements were done in a random fashion, throughout the 17 municipalities in the Skopje region. To achieve a balanced engagement among all the municipalities, the client USAID decided to conduct the assessment on the streets in person.
The 199 participants in the survey, as representatives, reflect the culture of the community in a smaller version.

Skopje 2009 assessment
199 people were involved, from 17 municipalities
Demographic picture

Employed in:		Number of assessed by Municipality:		Numbers by Age group:	
Public sector	56	Aerodrom	12	18-25 years	56
private sector	74	Aracinovo	10	26-40 years	79
NGO	7	Butel	16	41-65 years	55
Students	36	Cair	14	65+ years	9
Unemployed	13	Centar	13		
Retired	13	Cucer Sandevo	10		
		Gazi Baba	13		
		Gjorce Petrov	11		
Ethnicity:		Ilinden	10	Gender:	
		Karpos	13		
Macedonian	129	Kisela Voda	12	Male 110	
Albanians	46	Petrovec	12	Female 89	
Other	24	Saraj	11		
		Sopiste	10		
		Studenicani	10		
		Suto Orizari	10		
		Zelenikovo	10		
		Other	2		

Picture 1.10: Demographic picture of Skopje 2009 assessment

Results of measurement: 1 – Big gap in values

Among all 199 responses to each question, the 10 most common values floated to the top. These values are presented in the graphical results below.

The first column represents the values most appreciated by Macedonians in their personal lives.

The second column represents the values most frequently identified in Macedonia's current culture.

The third column represents the values that are most desired for the future, and signals the path towards the change wanted by the system, and not by individuals.

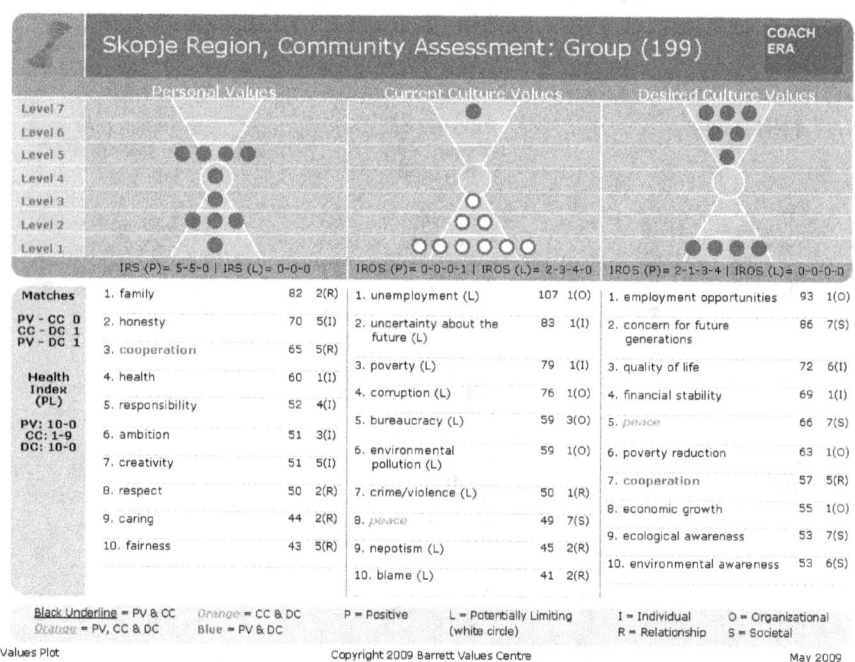

Picture 1.11: Key diagram from the 2009 Skopje measurement

In the pages that follow, in the section titled "**The full report**", the original assessment made by the Barrett Values Centre is presented, including all the recommendations made.

To begin with, let me explain in a few simple points the most important things visible in the diagram above.

The three images at the top show the values (circles) against the seven levels of consciousness. The dark circles represent **positive values**. The white circles represent the **limiting values**.

The first column is based on the question, "**Which 10 values best describe who you are (not who you want to be)?**" Here, the top position is taken by the most frequently chosen value among Macedonians in their personal lives, the value of **FAMILY**. In the same line the number "82" denotes the number of citizens (participants in the assessment) who chose this value. Next to this, the number 2 indicates the level of consciousness and motivation from which this value comes. This most important value is followed by the values of **honesty, cooperation, health, responsibility, ambition, creativity, respect, caring and fairness.**

The second column gives the answer to the question, "**Which 10 values describe the current functioning of your municipality-town?**" This column represents the reality in the current Macedonian culture, as perceived by the collective eye of the citizens. Here among the top 10 values, 9 are limiting, and represent the **pain in the functioning of current Macedonian society.**

UNEMPLOYMENT was selected by 107 citizens. This is a limiting value from the first level of consciousness and motivation. This is followed by the values of **uncertainty about the future, poverty, corruption, bureaucracy, environmental pollution, crime/violence, nepotism,** and **blame.** The only positive value in the current culture is **Peace.**

The third column, an answer to the question "**Which 10 values would you most like to see in your municipality-town?**" represents the most desirable values that citizens of Macedonia want to see in their society. The results in this column can be viewed as the **collectively intelligent direction** in which citizens want their system to develop. **Employment opportunities** is a value selected by 92 citizens, followed by **concern for future generations, quality of life, financial stability, peace, poverty reduction,** cooperation, economic growth, ecological awareness and environmental awareness.

Results of measurement: 2 - Low levels of alignment

The assessment diagram (Picture 1.11) also shows that at the moment of measurement (2009), Macedonian society functions at a very low level of **cohesion - alignment**. This is determined by the number of values that are repeated in two or all three columns; in the diagram, this is indicated with the word **matches** (on the left hand side).

The first column, **Personal Values (PV)**, does not align with the second column, **Current Culture (CC)**, with any value.
The second column, **CC**, aligns with the third column, **Desired Culture (DC)**, with only one value, **peace**.
The third column, **DC**, aligns with the first column, **PV**, with the value of **cooperation**.

If you observe corporation Macedonia as a team or organization, the above low levels of alignment indicate that the Macedonian community is divided and its values are misaligned, and this makes the system very inefficient.

This also means that the values that citizens most highly respect and possess in their personal lives (first column) cannot be fully manifested in society – these values and their positive energy are simply unsupported and blocked by the limiting values and behaviors in our current culture (second column). Because of this, the community is unhappy and frustrated, and wants a change in a new direction (third column).

The research done by the Barrett Values Center, which is based on the experiences that come from fieldwork done by the CTT consultants with their clients from all over the world, shows that organizations and communities with a healthy culture are characterized by a high degree of alignment. In some of the best cases, the alignment index shows six or more overlapping values between the current and desired culture.

An example of such an organization is one of South Africa's largest banks – Nedbank. They have begun a culture transformation effort by measuring their culture for the first time in 2005.

Nedbank: Current Culture Evolution

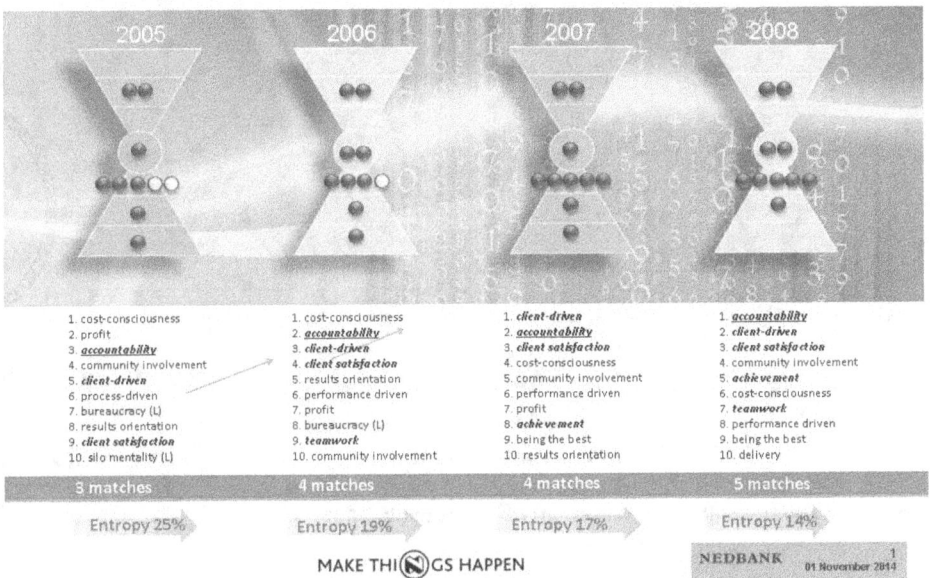

Picture 1.12A: The culture transformation at Nedbank, 2005-2012

When Nedbank started the process of cultural transformation in 2005, the bank had two limiting values in their current culture, and the alignment between the first column (employees' personal values) and second column (the organizational culture) was with three values. Through the process of cultural transformation, in just four years, the alignment evolved to a remarkable degree of cohesion – six values matched in 2009. The case study of this remarkable process was written by none other than the CEO of Nedbank himself – Tom Boardman[5].

---

[5] http://www.valuescentre.com/uploads/2011-01-05/The%20Nedbank%20Turnaround%20-%20The%20Tom%20Boardman%20Story.pdf

Nedbank: Current Culture Evolution

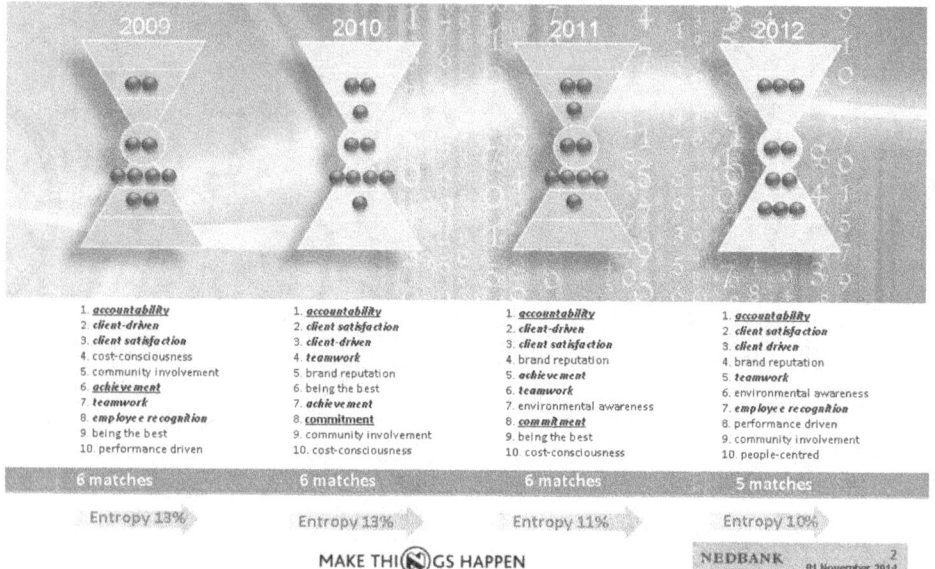

Picture 1.12B: The culture transformation at Nedbank, 2005-2012

Additionally, in order to emphasize the importance of the degree of alignment, and the impact of the limiting values on the operation and performance of any system or organization, take a look at the table below:

The impact of limiting values and the degree of alignment	
Alignment between the current (column II) and desired culture (column III)	
6 or more values	Excellent and healthy culture.
4-5, good	The group is on the right track.
2-3, in order	The group is close to the right track, but more work is needed.
0-1, weak	The group is unhappy and/or frustrated, and wants a change in a new direction.
Alignment between personal values (column I) and current culture (column II)	
3-4 values	People are able to be themselves at work / in society.
1-2	People can, with effort, be themselves at work / in society.
0	People are not able to be themselves at work / in society.
The presence of limiting values and their impact	
0 limiting values (LV)	This group does not operate from a place of fear.
1-2 LV	There may be some element of fear behind the decisions and the way the group is managed.
3 or more LV	Fear is a strong factor in this group and affects how it is managed.

Picture 1.13: The impact of limiting values and the degree of alignment

Results of measurement: 3 - High entropy

Cultural entropy is the amount of energy in an organization that is consumed in unproductive work. It is a measure of the conflict, friction and frustration that exist within an organization.

Barrett Values Centre

In mechanics, entropy is defined as the non-productive, negative energy that slows down the mechanism and thus creates losses. The simplest example of entropy is the motor engine of an old vehicle. Because of wear, the lack of lubrication or dirt, the old motor runs slower than a new one and has more entropy.

In the organizational and/or national context, entropy is a result of the limiting values and behaviors within the system. It only appears in the first three levels of consciousness.

The CTT tools measure entropy in percentages.

ORGANIZATIONAL entropy = $\dfrac{\text{Limiting values}}{\text{Total number of values}}$

In society, a simple example of entropy will be seen when attempting to get a document or permission from a clerk in the public administration. If you get the document at a single counter by dealing with one person, your work will be complete in 30 minutes.
If you need to get the same permission by dealing with a few counters and several different institutions in different buildings, and perhaps by making a call to a friend or acquaintances, to get what you are entitled to receive; or in an extreme situation, if you are being blackmailed by a civil servant who sabotages you because he is in favor of his cousin's proposal rather than yours; or if you have been asked for a bribe; then the time and energy you spend on this task becomes greater and more frustrating. This is how entropy manifests in the system.
In the case I just described, the entropy is manifested in the form of limiting values such as corruption, nepotism and bureaucracy.

The only way for an organization or nation to discover its own entropy is to measure its values and culture – otherwise the entropy remains invisible and questionable.

"If you can't measure, you can't manage"

In May 2009, the corporation Macedonia had a high 48% entropy in its current culture (column 2), spread across the first three levels of consciousness. The first level, survival, has 25%; the second level, relationships, has 12%; and the third level, self-esteem, has 11% entropy.

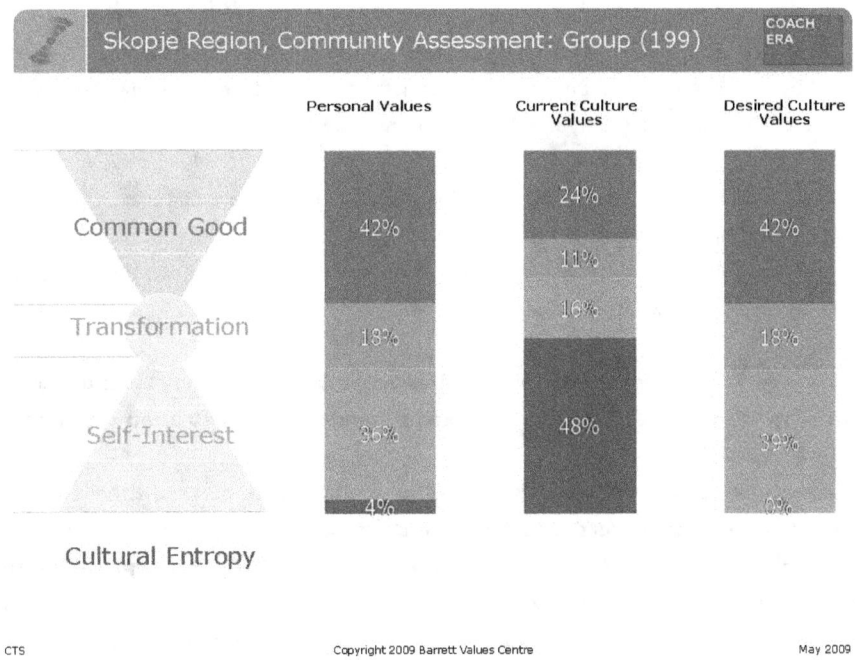

Picture 1.14: The entropy of the Macedonian community

Especially worrisome is the first level of consciousness, which has 25% of entropy. This is a quarter of the total energy of the system, and it is being wasted by the limiting values of **unemployment, uncertainty about the future, poverty, corruption, environmental pollution, and crime/violence.**

48% entropy, simply put, means that almost every other day in corporation Macedonia is unproductive, wasted, and lost.
When we translate this into money, the figures are simply shocking.

If the estimates made at the Barrett Values Centre for their clients are used in the Macedonian case, then for every 100 MKD (Macedonian Denar – the currency) that the state provides to pay for its administration, 48 denars are lost, from the very beginning of the budgetary calculations. Now according to the national budget for 2012, for the salaries of the administration, 370 million euros have been allocated. **48% of this money, or 177.6 million euros, are lost when the budget is adopted.**
Just as a measurement of the damage that Macedonia has taken from its entropy, I will compare this figure with the Foreign Direct Investments (FDI) in the same year. The data provided by the EBRD (European Bank for Reconstruction and Development) shows that in 2012, the country attracted only €100 million in inward FDI.[6]

If these estimates are true, then the 9 limiting values in the current culture: unemployment, uncertainty about the future, poverty, corruption, bureaucracy, environmental pollution, crime/violence, nepotism and blame, would have the following financial impact on corporation Macedonia:

- **48% of the salaries for the public administration are lost at any time of the functioning of the state. This figure makes the public administration expensive and inefficient.**
- **Organizations, businesses, and the state as a whole lose 48% of their energy, productivity, and the gross domestic product. Macedonia's GDP, according to the World Bank, in 2010 was USD 11,000,000,000 ($11 billion). This represents only 52% of Macedonian productivity.**
Based on the same estimates and data from the Barrett Values Centre that were originally used to calculate losses in the organizational context, and under the assumption that the state would have an entropy of 0%, the Macedonian GDP would be USD 21.15 billion.

---

[6] http://tr.ebrd.com/tr13/en/country-assessments/1/fyr-macedonia

> The bottom line according to these estimates is that every year, due to the limiting behaviors in the culture, corporation Macedonia loses USD 10.15 billion.

The challenge for Macedonian leaders, and for the country as a whole, is to create an aligned nation with a cohesive and innovative culture, which will be a desirable and rewarding place to live for all the Macedonian citizens (including those who are currently living abroad).

0% entropy is an impossible phenomenon, but an organization or community still functions very well when its entropy level is 10% or below. The functioning above this level of entropy comes with certain increasing risks for the system, as the table shows:

Organizational Entropy and the risks for the system

Less than 10%: Healthy functioning

11% - 20%: Problems that require attention and careful monitoring

21% - 30%: Serious problems that require immediate attention

31% - 40%: A crisis that requires urgent change

Above 41%: Present risk of bankruptcy, systemic collapse

Picture 1.15: The risks of organizational entropy

The creation of alignment in organizations and nations throughout the globe, according to the calculations that come from the companies and clients of the Barrett Values Center (see table below), could bring humankind incredible benefits and save the global economy spectacular financial figures measuring thousands of trillions of dollars.
Estimations show that because of limitations within their culture, the USA lose more

money than their annual GDP.

The price of entropy over the national GDP's

	National GDP in $US,000	Measured entropy	Calculated loss in the national economy $US,000
USA	14, 200, 000, 000	58%	19, 609, 000, 000
UK	2, 650, 000, 000	43%	1, 999, 000, 000
Canada	1, 400, 000, 000	32%	658, 000, 000
Belgium	498, 000, 000	53%	561, 000, 000
Sweden	454, 000, 000	31%	216, 000, 000
Venezuela	314, 000, 000	72%	807, 000, 000
Denmark	312, 000, 000	21%	83, 000, 000
Finland	238, 000, 000	48%	219, 000, 000
Latvia	27, 000, 000	54%	32, 000, 000
Island	20, 000, 000	54%	24, 000, 000

This numbers are based on the calculations made in the client companies using the CTT. They are based on the staff's perception of lost productivity and opportunity. Further research is being done in this direction.

Picture 1.16: The cost of entropy in the GDP of some nations

The high entropy in the Macedonian system reduces the systemic immunity, and makes the community very vulnerable to stressful systemic situations (economic and/or ethnic crises), which may have catastrophic consequences as in the case of the 2001 conflict.

Results of measurement: 4 - Strategy for growth and development not supported by the current culture

Experts in organizational development who are familiar with this subject, and who understand the importance of culture and its impact on the strategies of a company, often say:

> "Culture eats strategy for breakfast."

This means that when a strategy is not supported by and not aligned with the culture of an organization and the behaviors of the people, the chances of it being successfully implemented reduce significantly.

Phil Clothier, the CEO of the Barrett Values Centre, describes this in a simple way:

- Outstanding culture + Bad strategy = Entertainment in the first 10 minutes, and then we have no money.

- **Excellent strategy + Bad culture = Excluded and disengaged people, filled with stress, who do not have the energy to achieve basic goals.**

- **Outstanding culture + Excellent strategy = Involved and energized people, living with a common vision and values.**

We can see strategy and culture as the two key pillars that together carry the weight of a house. The strategy gives structure to the building, and culture provides the energy required to lift the house. When one does not support the other, there arises a common difficulty from which many organizations suffer.

Corporation Macedonia in recent times suffers from the second case:

- **Excellent strategy + Bad culture = Excluded and disengaged people, filled with stress, who do not have the energy to achieve basic goals.**

Let me illustrate this with two real examples from the current situation:

1) The development of tourism in Macedonia

During the last 5-7 years, the Macedonian government has made tremendous efforts and allocated substantial funds to promote Macedonia as a tourist destination, especially on the big worldwide television networks. Investments have been made in the two international airports, in the capital Skopje, and in the tourist towns of Ohrid/Struga (**this is part of the strategy**).
The low-cost carrier WIZZ Air has entered the Macedonian market and become the busiest carrier to and from Macedonia, connecting the country with direct destinations like never before.

The ad campaign launched in 2007 gave the first successful results very quickly. According to the state statistical office figures for the number of tourists, 2011 was an extraordinarily successful tourist season[7]. The Dutch, traditionally the biggest visitors from Western Europe, again visited Ohrid in large numbers.

Looking at these results, you could say to yourself, "Well, the goals have been reached, so isn't the strategy a success?"

But for a moment pay attention to the limiting value which occupies the 6th place in Macedonia's current culture – **Environmental pollution**. In reality, this value is manifested in millions of plastic bags strewn throughout the country. Plastic bottles and cans on the beaches of the lakes and in the forests, landfills around the mountain villages, and garbage without control…

The Dutch are among the leading nations in the world when it comes to the culture of environmental awareness.
How does our behavior towards the environment affect the Dutch tourists and their sense of well-being – And at the bottom line, how much are they willing to pay and spend for experience of this kind?
How well will they promote Macedonia once they return to Holland? Will they come back or recommend this destination to their fellow Dutchmen?

---

[7] http://www.stat.gov.mk/OblastOpsto.aspx?id=25

The Dutch, Finnish and for that matter, many Balkan guests will not sit and drink wine close to a landfill. Would you? If you ask me personally, I would not find this enjoyable and would not drink fine wine in these conditions.

One place below the value of environmental pollution, in the 7th place in the current culture, is the limiting value of crime/violence, which in the context of tourism, culminated in the violent murder of a foreign (Serbian citizen) tourist in Ohrid in 2010. The echoes from the murder and the subsequent trial had a dramatic impact and reduced the number of Serbian visitors in the following years. (Serbian tourists were otherwise the biggest regional visitors to Macedonia from the Balkan region.)

Don't get me wrong, I know my country. Macedonia is beautiful destination with magic to offer, but instead of maximizing the profits from the strategy and the investments in attracting new guests, our limiting values and behavior **(this is the culture)** have brought the excellent (5 stars) to an average level (2-3 stars). This is how Macedonians devalue their own tourism, and the energy invested in it.

The ultimate math, again, is money. Instead of charging premium rates for our tourism services, because of our limiting behaviors, these services come at a much cheaper price on the competitive and conscious market. This is how our culture eats our profits and undermines the strategy, in the field of tourism.

According to many, 2013 is considered as one of worst seasons in Ohrid in the past few years[8].

2) Strategies to attract foreign direct investment (FDI)

In the same way as with tourism, much has been invested in the promotion of and preparation for foreign investment. Some results are already visible. However, Macedonia has seen no difference in the increase in FDI as compared to the past, or in comparison with the neighboring countries, or the countries of South-East Europe. Percentages show that the FDI index is where it was before.

If you look again at the measurement of values and the current culture, it will be easy to understand why we remain where we were with respect to FDI: Corruption, bureaucracy, crime/violence, and nepotism.

---

[8] http://www.makdenes.org/content/article/25060251.html

These limiting values are dynamite for the demolition of many good strategies that corporation Macedonia has developed, including the strategy used to attract greater FDI. These values are not visible to the naked eye, but are felt on a subtle level. Especially alert and sensitive to them are those who need to put their money and labor as investments in Macedonia.

I strongly believe that if we support the strategies for attracting foreign direct investment with a transformation of our national culture, and especially with new strong leadership values, we will see the success of this and any other strategy, showing results in a much more positive direction. If we do not do this, Macedonians will be chasing their tails for a much longer time.

FULL ASSESSMENT

I will now present the full assessment of Skojpe in 2009 in its original form, as delivered by the Barrett Values Centre in 2009.

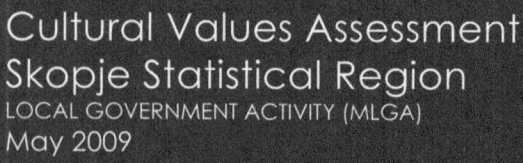

USAID | MACEDONIA
FROM THE AMERICAN PEOPLE

Cultural Values Assessment
Skopje Statistical Region
LOCAL GOVERNMENT ACTIVITY (MLGA)
May 2009

May 2009
This publication is prepared for United States Agency for International Development. The assessment was prepared by Barrett Values Centre and Coach Era Group, employed by ARD, Inc. which is implementing USAID/MLGA Project.

Prepared by: Barrett Values Centre, www.valuescentre.com : +1 828 252 5555
Project Consultant: Coach Era Group, www.skyisthelimit.org

Contact:
Viktor Kunovski,
MD Coach Era Group
www.skyisthelimit.org
viktor@skyisthelimit.org
Tel: +44 (0)7722018842
    +389 (0)70 991320

For USAID/MLGA:
Rozalija Karchicka – Vasilevska M.Sc, Local Economic Development Team Leader, USAID/ Macedonian Local Government Activity.

Copyright © 2009. All rights reserved. This document cannot be completely or partially translated or copied without publisher's permission. Any storage or archiving, electronic adjustments, computer programming or use with any similar or different technology known today or to be developed in future shall be forbidden.

Виктор Куновски
© КОУЧ ЕРА 2011
www.skyisthelimit.org/mk.htm

Table of Contents

Executive Summary
Section 1
  Personal Values
  Current Culture Values
  Current Entropy
  Desired Culture Values
  Distribution of All Values
  Positive Values by Level
  Values Jumps

Section 2
  Recommendations

Overview

CURRENT STRENGTHS of Skopje Statistical Region

The **Personal Values** of the people in the Skopje Statistical Region show that they demonstrate:

- Openness and support in their relationships
- Being dependable and having a strong drive to realise their goals
- Envisioning different approaches to living and being
- Taking care of themselves and others in their lives

Their top value is "family". They also have a high number of "relationship" type **values**. This shows that people and their connections to them are notably important in their lives.

Their values are concentrated at level 5. This shows that they seek purpose and meaning in their life experiences.

The **Current Culture** of the community is driven by values that promote:

- Chronic problems at the survival level
- Fears about safety
- Unfair and illegal business practices
- Lack of clarity about the direction of the community

There is only one positive value: peace.

Clearly, the people in the community are frustrated and concerned about present conditions and behaviours.

The entropy is 48%, which indicates severe dysfunction. Entropy at this level is unsustainable for the future and it must be reduced in order to avoid further social unrest and potential financial consequences.

THE WAY FORWARD FOR Skopje Statistical Region

The people surveyed want to retain their community focus on "peace".
They have chosen nine new values that focus on building a more solid foundation or fiscal growth.

The people want to live in a community that produces opportunities for work and considers the long term impact on people and their environment.

They want the community to protect the most fragile in the community, the elderly and the disadvantaged.
There is a stronger focus on "societal" type values, showing that they want their community to be guided by principles that support the common good.
Note that while the distribution of all values shows that there are values at levels 3 and 4, the areas of systems and process and continuous renewal, there are no top values represented in the Desired Culture. This shows that there is focus in this area but little consensus around which values should be driving change. It may be helpful to talk about these levels with people to get more clarity on which values would support change at these levels.

Section 1
Skopje Statistical Region

Section 1: Personal Values

Personal Values in Order of Predominance		
	Vote	Level
family	82	2
honesty	70	5
cooperation	65	5
health	60	1
responsibility	52	4
ambition	51	3
creativity	51	5
respect	50	2
caring	44	2
fairness	43	5

Top

PL= 10-0
IRS (P)= 5-5-0
IRS (L)= 0-0-0

P - Positive
L - Potentially Limiting
I - Individual
R - Relationship
S - Societal
○ Potentially Limiting
● Positive Value

199 Participants

What is important to the people of Macedonian Community?
*From an analysis of the Personal Values chosen by the people in your community, we can learn what are the principal values that unite them and what they collectively draw from when making decisions in their lives (Top Values). We can also see how their values are distributed across the Seven Levels of Consciousness Model (All Values). Every value chosen can be classified as an Individual, Relationship or Societal Value (**IRS**).*

Key themes from Top Values

- Openness and support in their relationships
- Being dependable and having a strong drive to realise their goals
- Taking care of themselves and others in their lives

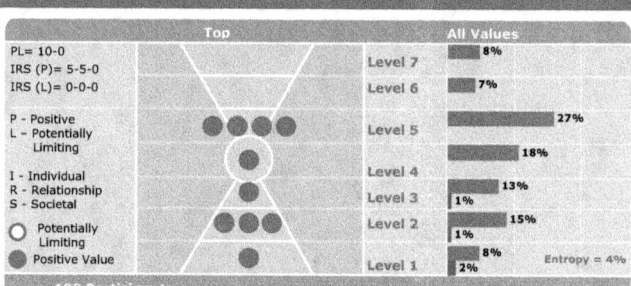

Values Concentration

- In the top Personal Values the values are located in five of the seven levels with concentration at level 5 - Internal Cohesion. This concentration shows that many of the people in this group have a focus on finding life's mission and meaning.

- When we look at all of the values chosen we also see the most focus at level 5 - Internal Cohesion (27%). Level 5 represents personal cohesion, maturity and/or a search for meaning. The distribution of all values shows where the most energy is concentrated for this group, not just where there is consensus on specific values.

Section 1: Personal Values TC "Personal Values" \l 2 (continued)

Values Gaps

A values gap occurs where one or more of the seven levels has no top values. This can mean one of three things; that the levels a) are unconsciously taken care of, b) are a blind spot, or c) represent the next area of growth.

There are no top positive values in the following levels:

Level 6 - Making a difference focuses on creating positive change through awareness and contribution from a personal and community perspective

Level 7 - Service reflects the highest order of internal and external connectedness

It is important to check the 'All Values' chart at the levels where there are no top values to see if the percentage of total votes at that level is significant. A high percentage at a level with no top values indicates that there is focus in this area but there is little agreement as to which values are important.

Values Types

- **IRS:** Of the top positive values chosen five are individual values, five are relationship values and none are societal values. It is common in the personal values to see a concentration of "individual" type values. However, this group shows a high number of relationship values as well, showing that people and their connections to them are significant in their lives.

57

Section 1: Current Culture Values

Current Culture Values in Order of Predominance	Vote	Level
unemployment (L)	107	1
uncertainty about the future (L)	83	1
poverty (L)	79	1
corruption (L)	76	1
bureaucracy (L)	59	3
environmental pollution (L)	59	1
crime/violence (L)	50	1
peace	49	7
nepotism (L)	45	2
blame (L)	41	2

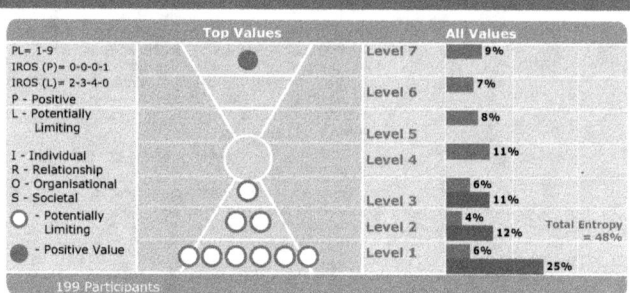

PL= 1-9
IROS (P)= 0-0-0-1
IROS (L)= 2-3-4-0
P - Positive
L - Potentially Limiting
I - Individual
R - Relationship
O - Organisational
S - Societal
○ - Potentially Limiting
● - Positive Value

199 Participants

What is shaping participants' experience?

The Current Culture Values reflect the participants' perceptions of their community and the day-to-day environment in which they live and work – both the positive aspects of their experiences, and the potential problem areas. In addition to the values types listed for the personal values (IRS) we now also have Organisational type values. (IROS)

Key themes from Top Values
- Chronic problems at the survival level
- Fears about safety
- Unfair and illegal business practices
- Lack of clarity about the direction of the community

Values Concentration

- In the Current Culture, the top values are distributed in four of the seven levels with concentration at level 1, showing that much of the energy goes toward survival needs. However, nearly all of the values are limiting and draining resources and energy from growth and development in this area.

- When we look at all of the values, both positive and potentially limiting, we can see that the highest focus for this community is also at level 1 - Survival (31%). Level 1 represents financial stability and the safety and security of the people in the community. As noted, the vast majority of this focus in from limiting values.

Section 1: Current Culture Values TC " Current Culture Values " \l 2 (continued)

Values Gaps

There are no top positive values in the following levels:

Level 1 - Survival focuses on financial matters and community growth

Level 2 - Relationship focuses on interpersonal relationships

Level 3 - Self-esteem focuses on performance, systems and processes

Level 4 - Transformation focuses on renewal and development

Level 5 - Internal Cohesion focuses on building a sense of united spirit inside the community

Level 6 - Making a difference on creating mutually beneficial partnerships both inside and outside of the community

Values Types

- **IROS:** Of the top positive values chosen none are individual values, none are relationship values, none are organisational values and one is a societal value. This shows that the people see little positive focus in the community.

Values Matches: Personal and Current Culture

Matching values indicate alignment. The greater the number of matching Personal and Current Culture values, the greater the degree to which people are likely to feel a strong sense of connection between their personal values and their community environment.
In a highly aligned culture, one would expect to see three or four matching Personal and Current Culture values.
There are no matching values.
No values matches indicate that the people in your community are not aligned with the values of the current culture. This lack of alignment reduces the level of engagement people feel to their community, creates frustration and breeds disillusionment.

Section 1: Current Entropy

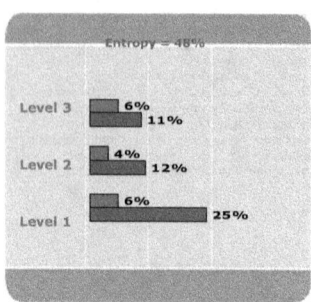

Level	Potentially Limiting Values (votes)	Percentage Entropy
3	bureaucracy (59) illiteracy (40) pessimism (37) centralized government (35) elitism (20) wasted resources (18) strict moral/religious codes (14)	223 out of 351: 11% of total votes
2	nepotism (45) blame (41) hatred (35) conflict/aggression (33) tradition (31) isolation (30) ethnic discrimination (18) gender discrimination (14)	247 out of 331: 12% of total votes
1	unemployment (107) uncertainty about the future (83) poverty (79) corruption (76) environmental pollution (59) crime/violence (50) short-term focus (30) materialistic (16) terrorism (7)	507 out of 622: 25% of total votes

Potentially Limiting Values create cultural entropy. Entropy is a measure of the degree of dysfunction in a system and represents the proportion of votes for potentially limiting values. The chart shows the percentage of potentially limiting values in the Current Culture. Potentially limiting values are found only at levels 1, 2 and 3. The table shows the specific issues contributing to the entropy at each level. Entropy levels of 10 percent or lower indicate a healthy community.

48% of all votes were for potentially limiting values. **This is an alarmingly high level of entropy indicating**

potential financial collapse and social unrest. Immediate consideration should be given to cultural and structural transformation and leadership development.
- There are nine potentially limiting values in the top values of the Current Culture. What are the causes and corrective actions behind these values?

Unemployment leads to poverty and can propagate a downward economic spiral

Uncertainty about the future can stifle growth and investment and lead to

Section 1: TC "Current Entropy" \ I 2 Current Entropy (continued)

excessive caution in making long-term decisions.

Poverty undermines the economic and social resilience of a nation. It undermines economic development by making it difficult to establish and develop domestic markets. It undermines social development by reducing the Government's access to funds through taxation.

Corruption is an indicator that there is more focus on self-interest than the common good. Corruption generates economic inefficiencies and makes it difficult for businesses to prosper.

Bureaucracy makes it difficult for businesses to thrive, and also makes it difficult for citizens to access the public services they may need.

Environmental pollution undermines the health of the community and the ability for earth to sustain life.

Crime/violence indicates that people fear for their basic security and safety.

Nepotism creates an unfair system in which people are not hired based on competency but on their relationship to their employer. This breeds resentment and possible places power in the hands of those less competent.

Blame depicts a fear-based culture where people avoid taking responsibility for their actions and project their mistakes onto others.

Concentration of Entropy

- The entropy is concentrated at Level 1 indicating severe problems in how this community meets survival needs.

Key themes

- Lack of safety and protection for the citizens of the community
- Unfair and slow moving business practices
- Lack of opportunities for work and lack of basic survival needs for many in the population
- Lack of protection for the environment and the next generation

61

Section 1: Desired Culture Values

Desired Culture Values in Order of Predominance		
	Vote	Level
employment opportunities	93	1
concern for future generations	86	7
quality of life	72	6
financial stability	69	1
peace	66	7
poverty reduction	63	1
cooperation	57	5
economic growth	55	1
ecological awareness	53	7
environmental awareness	53	6

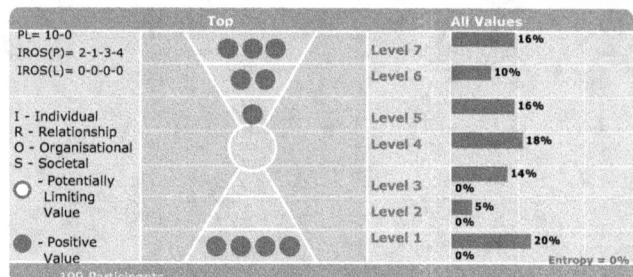

PL= 10-0
IROS(P)= 2-1-3-4
IROS(L)= 0-0-0-0

I - Individual
R - Relationship
O - Organisational
S - Societal

○ - Potentially Limiting Value
● - Positive Value

199 Participants

All Values
- Level 7: 16%
- Level 6: 10%
- Level 5: 16%
- Level 4: 18%
- Level 3: 14% / 0%
- Level 2: 5% / 0%
- Level 1: 20% / 0%

Entropy = 0%

What values do participants want for their future?

The Desired Culture Values reflect what participants believe to be important for the well being of the community. These values provide a road map to the future by identifying possible antidotes to current problems and values that need strengthening.

Key Themes from Top Values

- Stabilising bottom line needs for shelter and work
- Effective stewardship that protects the earth and accounts for those who come after us
- People working together
- Creating a meaningful and fulfilling environment where people can thrive

Values Matches: Current Culture and Desired Culture

Matching values indicate alignment. The greater the number of matching Current and Desired Culture values, the greater the degree to which people believe the community is on the right track.

There is one matching value:

peace

This is the attribute that this group experiences now and wants to continue to support in the future. One to three values matches shows that the people have some confidence in the current direction of your community yet want to see a significant shift in values that will elevate and strengthen their environment.

Section 1: TC "Desired Culture Values" \I 2 Desired Culture Values (continued)

Values Matches: Personal Values and Desired Culture
There is one matching value:
  cooperation

This is a value that, if chosen to be a guiding principle of this community, could easily be brought to work by this group, as it is important in their daily lives.

Across-the-board Matches
There are no across-the-board matching values between the Personal, Current and Desired Culture values.

New Values in the Desired Culture
These are values in the Desired Culture Values list that are not in the Current Culture Values list. They are values that the respondents would like to see implemented in order for your community to beocome higher funsctioning.
There are nine new values in the values plot diagram.
  employment opportunities
  concern for future generations
  quality of life
  financial stability
  poverty reduction
  cooperation
  economic growth
  ecological awareness
  environmental awareness

Values Concentration
- In the Desired Culture, the top values are distributed in four of the seven levels with concentration at Level 1, showing that the participants want energy devoted to financial matters and community growth.

- When we look at all of the values chosen we can see that the focus for this community is at level 1 - Survival (20%). Level 1 represents financial stability and the safety and security of the people in the community.

Values Gaps
There are no top positive values in the following levels:

Level 2 - Relationship focuses on interpersonal relationships either internally or externally, or both

Level 3 - Self-esteem focuses on performance, systems and processes

Level 4 - Transformation focuses on renewal and development

The 'All Values' percentages indicate how much focus participants feel there needs to be in each of these areas overall.

Values Types
- **IROS:** Of the top positive values chosen two are individual values, one is a relationship value, three are organisational values and four are societal values. This shows that people want the community to promote values that will serve the common good.

63

Section 1: Distribution of All Values

The Distribution of Values diagrams show the percentage of votes for values in three major areas - "Self Interest," "Transformation" and "Common Good." "Self Interest" is represented by levels 1, 2 and 3, and encompasses our basic needs, such as financial and physical health, interpersonal relationships, and systems and processes that support our individual and communityal needs. "Transformation" is represented by level 4. This level is about giving people a voice, beginning to challenge and question ideas, and embracing opportunities for growth and learning. "Common Good" encompasses levels 5, 6 and 7. In these levels, individuals and communitys are focused on the well-being of the collective, finding meaning in their lives and work, and how they can support others in building a long-term sustainable future.

	Personal Values	Current Culture Values	Current Culture Values	Desired Culture Values	Personal Values	Desired Culture Values
Common Good		24%	24%			
Transformation	42%	11%	11%	42%	42%	42%
Self-Interest	18%	16%	16%	18%	18%	18%
	36%	48%	48%	39%	36%	39%
Cultural Entropy	4%			0%	4%	0%

There is misalignment here between the make-up of the values people hold personally and those they currently experience in your community.

There is severe misalignment between the distribution of values people are currently experiencing and those they would like to see in the Desired Culture. This misalignment shows that they see a need to shift focus to meeting survival needs and serving the common good.

There is exact alignment between the group's personal values and the direction they are asking for in their Desired Culture, indicating that they have the energy to support the changes they are seeking.

Section 1: Positive Values by Level

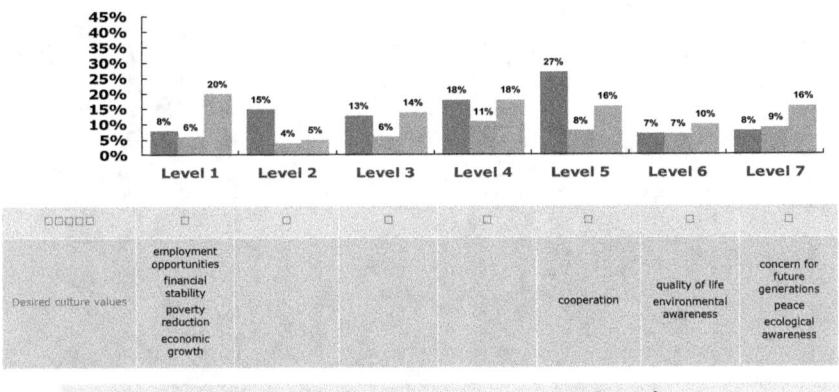

	Level 1	Level 2	Level 3	Level 4	Level 5	Level 6	Level 7
	☐	☐	☐	☐	☐	☐	☐
Desired culture values	employment opportunities financial stability poverty reduction economic growth				cooperation	quality of life environmental awareness	concern for future generations peace ecological awareness

This diagram shows the percentage of Personal, Current and Desired Culture votes for positive values by level. The table indicates the top Desired Culture values chosen by participants at the levels where they are requesting the most new focus. These are significant as they provide clarity around the desired direction of your organisation.

■ **Personal**

■ **Current Culture**

■ **Desired Culture**

Section 1: Values Jumps

This table shows the values that received the greatest increase in votes from the Current Culture to the Desired Culture. The values in **bold** are top values in the Desired Culture. These are values the participants consider need to be enhanced for the future well-being of the community.

Key Requests:
- Stabilising bottom line needs for shelter and work
- Providing support and protection for the most fragile in the community
- Effective stewardship that protects the earth and accounts for those who come after us

Value	Current Culture Votes	Desired Culture Votes	Jump
employment opportunities	27	93	66
financial stability	7	69	62
concern for future generations	32	86	54
poverty reduction	12	63	51
economic growth	6	55	49
quality of life	24	72	48
community pride	14	43	29
affordable housing	5	33	28
caring for the disadvantaged	8	35	27
equality	19	45	26
caring for the elderly	10	36	26
environmental awareness	28	53	25

Section 2
Recommendations

Section 2: Recommendations

These recommendations are based on your results and provide insights and questions to guide the future direction and success of your community.

- Develop a plan to deliver internal communication around these results. Consider setting up focus groups to gain greater understanding around specific areas or issues and planning steps for improvement.
- The cultural entropy in your community, 48%, needs to be reduced immediately, as it is alarmingly high. Identify the meaning and experiences that people see in the potentially limiting values of **unemployment, uncertainty about the future, poverty, corruption, bureaucracy, environmental pollution, crime/violence, nepotism**, and **blame**. Ask the participants what they see as the causes, limiting behaviours and negative results of each of these values, and the corrective actions that they or others might take. Consider doing a cost analysis of these values to see how they are impacting the community in terms of lost efficiency and productivity.
- Define the key areas your community will focus on in the next year. Develop specific actions and programs that will foster these changes. Consider repeating the survey process next year to gauge the progress you have made in these areas.

- Pay particular attention to any Personal Values that are being asked for in the Desired Culture. Talk to people about what these values mean to them and what they can do in order to better support these values in their workplace. Create programs of values integration so that the people can bring more of who they are and what they can offer to work.
- Look at the values gaps in the Current Culture –Do these signify a weakness in the community? Is there a strong call for values at these levels within the Desired Culture? Is there concentration of personal values associated with these levels?
- Examine the new values requested in the Desired Culture: **employment opportunities, concern for future generations, quality of life, financial stability, poverty reduction, cooperation, economic growth, ecological awareness,** and **environmental awareness**. Determine their meanings and

what changes in behavior are necessary to implement these values.
- Discuss how your community can continue to live the value of **peace**.
- Consider the values jumps in the Current Culture to Desired Culture - are there words that do not show up in the Desired Culture but seem significant considering the current situation in the community?

Back to corporation Macedonia

Corporation Macedonia currently has very serious problems.

This is evident from the diagnosis just presented. Not only does the corporation fail to function on the full spectrum of consciousness (does not drive balanced on the seven cylinders), but it is also "injured" at the first three levels of consciousness, with particularly serious trouble at the first level.

The limiting values in the culture can be compared with malignant cancerous cells in an organism. They create organizational illnesses that weaken and hurt the whole system (organization and/or nation).

In the business context, and in general, limiting values simply eat away your labor and create losses. This is not sustainable.

If corporation Macedonia wants to become a stable community and a quality place of living for its citizens, it will have to deal with the six limiting values on the first level (uncertainty about the future, poverty, corruption, environmental pollution, crime/violence). The corporation and its leadership must, in addition, find ways to neutralize the other limiting values in their culture (nepotism, bureaucracy and blame).

The ultimate goal is to create a nation that will be characterized by a high degree of alignment, minimal entropy, and an innovative culture.

The graph on the next page is named "**Leadership, Innovation, Co-Creation, Inspiration 2020**" and presents opportunities and potential for corporation Macedonia, as well as for other companies and nations, which are both realistic and achievable, if we follow the examples of successful companies that have already undertaken this kind of transformation.

In the example provided on the next page, the alignment between the first and second columns (personal values and current culture) is with six values.
Between the current culture and desired culture (the second and third columns), the alignment is five values.
The desired values and personal values (third column and first column) also align with five values.

Such a constellation would make corporation Macedonia an aligned community with explosive creativity, innovation, and performances that would exceed all previously known and achieved results.

Harmonized in such a way, corporation Macedonia will create economic results that we all desire, and achieve annual growth rates of more than 6-7%.

My belief is that if we achieve the proposed level of alignment, Macedonia will surpass a 10% annual GDP growth. This will automatically contribute to a better quality of life.

Leadership, Innovation, Inspiration, Co-creation 2020						
Personal values (PV)		Current culture (CC)		Desired culture (DC)		
1. family	2	1. Financial stability	1	1. Employment opportunities	1
2. leadership	6	2. respect	2	2. Future generations	7
3. cooperation	5	3. responsibility	4	3. Quality of life	6
4. health	1	4. cooperation	5	4. Financial stability	1
5. responsibility	4	5. excellence	3	5. vision	7
6. ambition	3	6. family	2	6. ambition	3
7. creativity	5	7. innovation	4	7. cooperation	5
8. respect	2	8. vision	7	8. respect	2
9. Future generations	7	9. creativity	5	9. responsibility	4
10. Ecological awareness	7	10. leadership	6	10. Regional collaboration	6

PV - CC 6
CC - DC 5
PV - DC 5

Health Index (PL)

PV: 10-0
CC: 10-0
DC: 10-0

Positive ●
Limiting ○

Black Underline = PV & CC   Orange = CC & DC
Orange = PV, CC & DC   Blue = PV & DC

Vision for Macedonia 2020

Picture 1.16: Leadership, Innovation, Co-Creation, Inspiration 2020: A vision of positive and aligned values for Macedonia

From this optimistic and positive perspective, I would like to ask a **KEY QUESTION:**

What will Macedonia look like, and how will life be in the country, if we achieve this level of alignment? How will it be if we move from Good to GREAT?

This is not a fantasy. The experiences of hundreds of large companies show that creating a strong and aligned culture is possible and viable for a period of 3 to 5 years.

The example of Unilever Brazil

Unilever Brazil is part of Unilever Corporation, a company with a strong reputation and 80 years of history. They have over 10,000 employees and annual sales of 3 billion euros, only in Brazil. For a comparative picture of how much money this is, let's just mention that the budget of Macedonia for 2012 amounted to 2.7 billion euros.

After several decades of strong growth, in 2004-05, the revenue of Unilever Brazil decreased. Kees Kruthof, CEO of Unilever Brazil, together with his team, launched a program to improve the performance and revenue. Apart from the strategic challenges and key management operations, the focus was placed on the organizational culture of the company. Unilever Brazil began to dream of what the company would look like when they became "Greater than Great".
At the beginning of this process, their CEO stated:

"**Unless we change our culture, we'll never achieve our highest business goals.**"

Kees Kruythoff
CEO, Unilever Brazil

The first measurement of Unilever Brazil's culture in 2008 showed 5 limiting values and 37% entropy. The second measurement, 12 months and several cultural leadership interventions after the initial one, the culture of Unilever underwent a visible change. The entropy decreased to 19% and the number of limiting values dropped to 2.

Unilever merged the management of the organizational culture with that of their strategy, and the culture became the pillar supporting the strategy.

Their commitment to this process goes so far, that the measurements of the culture are performed every 6 months (this is twice the frequency of once in 12 months proposed by the Barrett Values centre).

For those interested in learning in greater detail about the process of cultural transformation at Unilever Brazil and the consequent results, you can look at Unilever's experience through their case study[9].

In addition, here are the two slides from the first and subsequent measurements of the Unilever's culture.
The alignment has increased in this period, from 2-2-3 to 2-6-4[10] matches.

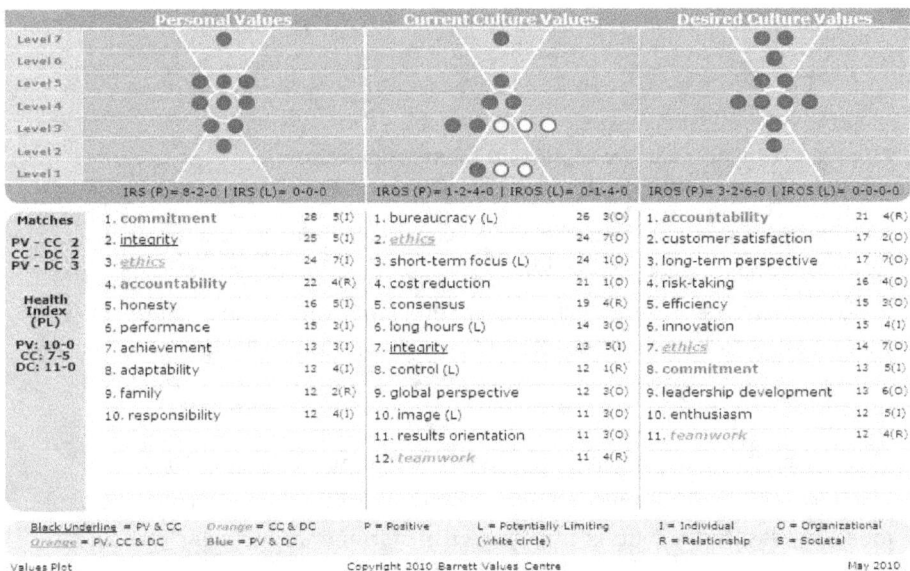

Picture 1.16: Unilever Brazil first measurement 2008

---

[9] http://www.valuescentre.com/uploads/2010-09-02/Unilever%20Brazil%20Case%20Study.pdf
[10] The alignment is marked with the word **matches visable on the left hand side**
PV – CC = 2, CC – DC = 2, PV –DC = 3.

73

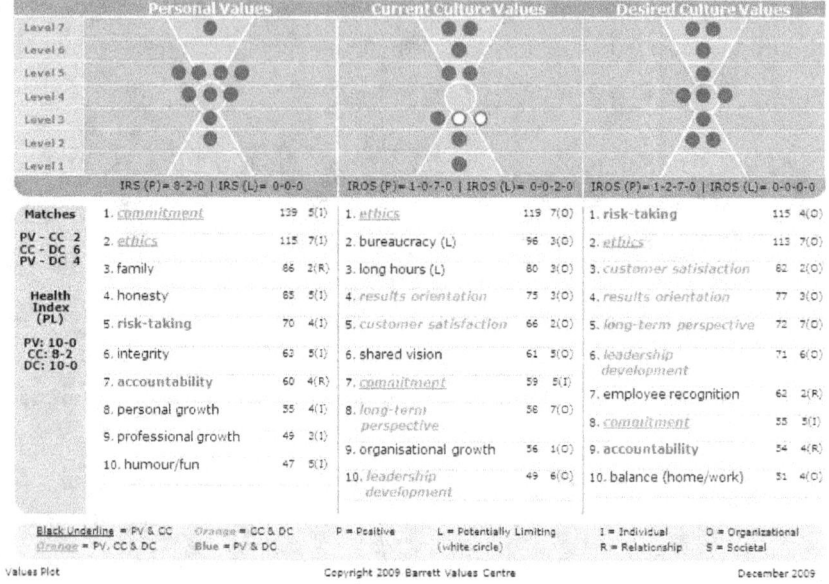

Picture 1.17: Unilever Brazil second measurement 2009

As a result of this improvement in the culture of Unilever, customer complaints have fallen from 31% in 2007 to 21% in 2009 (per million items sold). Client service measurements in completed cases, have improved from 71% in 2007 to 91% in 2009. Sales have grown from 3.2% per year (in the period 2002-07, before the transformation) to 7% per year in 2008-09.

If you are wondering about the parallel I make between transforming a company and transforming a community or a nation, it is interesting to mention that in the context of culture transformation, the principles and methods are identical for all types of organizations, and the only variable is the size of the system.

In addition, it is interesting to note that the "CTT" that are used for culture assessments were originally designed to help businesses measure and manage their culture. Once the companies had used them, and realized their amazing benefits, in the last decade larger systems such as administrative regions (Skopje-Macedonia, Extremadura-Spain and North West UK) and nations (Sweden[11], USA, Singapore, Australia, Switzerland, Latvia, to name just few) have started to use the CTT.

---

[11] Sweden has done 6 consecutive measurements since 2009/10/11/12/13/14/

The assessments used as diagnostic reports, in combination with powerful dialogic methods, are proving to provide an amazing platform for transformative cultural interventions for large groups. I will point to Australia[12] as a leader and example of dialogue on a national level, followed by Sweden[13].

Culture eats strategy for breakfast, AGAIN!

When in February 2009 I was called in for our first conversation, the senior project manager began with the following words:

...USAID has been operating in Macedonia for 20 years. We have done many good projects, yet we feel that we have not moved from the starting point...

This statement did not surprise me at all. Many Macedonian citizens share the same feeling, as if we have been standing still for the past 20 years.
If our leaders and the whole nation do not make serious changes in the culture of corporation Macedonia, the same feeling may remain for 20 years to come. Here is why.

In 2011, the consulting firm Deloitte published a report titled **Leadership Design**[14]. In it, one of the chapters has the intriguing title:
Culture eats strategy for breakfast... and leadership is just the starter.

What do they want to say with this provocative title?
They point out how business strategy is powerless in achieving the desired performance goals, unless it is supported by and aligned with the organizational culture.

The latest business experiences show that culture is crucial to the performance of an organization. On average, the culture is eight times more important than business strategy when it comes to performance.

---

[12] http://www.corpevolution.com/assets/Uploads/AI-Practitioner-Case-History-L-Doig-and-K-Muller-May-2011-Issue.pdf
[13]http://www.anpdm.com/newsletterweb/4244504B7342415B4575494159/41475D4A754640504B71414B5B4171
[14] http://www.deloitte.com/assets/Dcom-Kenya/Local%20Assets/Documents/Deloitte%20Report%20-%20Leadership%20by%20Design.pdf

As a matter of fact, the culture is so powerful and important, that when it is not in alignment with the business strategy, it is your greatest and most terrible enemy, stronger than any opponent in the market.

If we compare the experience of Unilever Brazil with that of corporation Macedonia, several conclusions can be drawn.
The ambitious plan and strategy of the Macedonian leadership is completely unsupported by the values of the sociopolitical leaders and the current culture in the nation. If we proceed in this way, there will be results, but they will stay within the frame of "good", and not reach the "GREAT", as pointed out with the two specific Macedonian examples of the tourism industry and foreign direct investment.
The economic facts state that corporation Macedonia actually needs more than good results. Studies and analysis suggest that with the current level of growth and development, Macedonia will take 80 years to reach the average level of development in the European Union.

!!! 80 years ? ? ?

Using the plainest of words, if we continue to behave in the same way as we have until now, if we continue to function from the comfort zone of old values and behaviors which clearly do not function well, we'll end up at a dead end.
This is not the case only for corporation Macedonia – this is true for many organizations and nations around the world.

A few words about the "good", and why it is the greatest enemy of the "GREAT"

If corporation Macedonia, its leaders, and its "employees" (citizens) are sincere in their intention to achieve their highest goals, they must focus on improving the organizational culture. The same transformation needs to be made by companies and institutions all over the country.

The golden key to a high level of creativity, innovation, and sustainable performance in the 21st century is an aligned and innovative organizational culture. This culture is your greatest ally, or your main

enemy if it is weak and misaligned.

The confirmation that a weak and misaligned culture is the number one enemy of your business or nation, is the number of companies that went bankrupt during the latest global economic crisis, which still continues to shake the planet. Many companies did not collapse because their competition outclassed or beat them in the market. Many companies collapsed because of their toxic culture and leadership that were dominated by limiting values.
The same happened to our southern neighbors, Greece, at the national level.

Unfortunately, the same thing can happen to corporation Macedonia, if our leaders and all of us do not make a serious commitment towards the change of our consciousness, values, and behavior.

PART II

How are we creating an exceptional, creative and innovative nation, with a high quality of life for our citizens and for future generations?

How are we creating an innovative culture that supports our strategies?

At the heart of this book is the question which is essential for Macedonian citizens, businesses, and the whole nation. My belief is that similar questions lie in the hearts and minds of leaders and people in many organizations, regions and nations.

How do we create a better-quality Macedonia, a comfortable, safe, creative, innovative and healthy place for all of us to live in?

Humanity has always striven to improve the quality of life. This progressive urge is perhaps one of the strongest evolutionary energies that move us every day on the planet. The question I posed above with regard to Macedonia can, on a wider scale, be formulated as:

How are we creating organizations, institutions and nations with exceptional and innovative cultures, which are in support of the highest goals of humanity?

As I mentioned before, the goal of an aligned culture is not just possible to attain – it might also be the key to what we call sustainable development.

The above key questions, as well as the other key questions that will be raised in the following pages, together with the transformation that they would generate, could save an estimated **10.15 billion** dollars annually for the corporation Macedonia (almost as much as the current GDP of the state).

The answer/s to such important questions cannot and must not come from one person or a small influential group of people. I will therefore not try to give any answers; my intention is rather to shine a light on how to find the best answers and solutions to the pressing challenges faced by my nation, many organizations, and humanity as a whole.

The answer to these questions can and need to come from the system as a whole. They need to be co-created, to reflect the collective intelligence of the system.

In order to create exceptional organizations and nations, and to respond to the enormous challenges confronting mankind in this millennium, in addition to creating an innovative organizational and national culture, we require a few **post conventional leadership practices**[15]:

1) Systemic Leadership and "Co-Creation"
2) Creative Dialogue
3) Presence

Before paying detailed attention to the above points, let's see how corporation Macedonia and humanity as a whole have reached the place where we are now. For this purpose, let's look at how the linear and autocratic management and/or leadership style that still dominates organizations around the world has come about.

We'll start from our western educational system, something we all know too well. Let's look at this from the perspective of psychological dynamics. The building of these complex dynamics begins in our classrooms.
A modern classroom has the teacher's desk, which is often at a higher level and is more massive than the students' desks. Facing the teacher's desk, the pupils or students are grouped together. The typical and most common classroom dynamics look like this:
The teacher or the professor is the one who knows – questions come to him/her, and s/he "answers" them. This exchange is often a monologue which is one-sided and subjective, and reflects the thoughts, values, and consciousness of one dominant person – the teacher. S/he tells or shows, and dominates the space and

---

[15] I use the word **practices** because these skills cannot be learned only from books, they need to be continuously practiced.

the time in the classroom. S/he has the power to evaluate, judge, punish. In a single word, s/he is the boss in the classroom.

Students, most of the time, are passive listeners. They are the ones who know less and who ask questions, needing the teacher's knowledge. They are evaluated, and may be punished for not knowing enough.
The psychological dynamics in the classroom are mostly between BIG (parent/teacher) and SMALL (child/student). The power is on the side of the teacher. The student, through such dynamics, cannot be empowered, because s/he doesn't have equal participation in the dynamics of the exchange in the first place.

These dynamics are later transferred to the workplace as a "copy and paste", in most organizations. The boss, the director, now occupies the role of the teacher: they manage the students, who are now the employees.
The boss gives orders, makes decisions, and often takes responsibility and control into his/her hands. S/he can punish or even fire the employee. Most of the time, the boss is expected to know and solve problems.
The employee is more than often the subordinate, like when s/he was a student. S/he is the passive receiver of orders about what and needs to be done and how. Since the employee is mostly told or ordered how to work, s/he doesn't assume full responsibility. If s/he makes a mistake, s/he can justify it with the excuse – "You told me to do so – to do it that way".

The dynamics remain intact in the political context. Authoritarian regimes, as well as many political systems in most developed democracies, often have similar authoritarian dynamics as the classroom or workplace.
The President, the Prime Minister, or the Mayor, just like the boss and the teacher, are the dominant, the knowing, the intelligent, the responsible ones. They make decisions about and on behalf of voters (the people). These decisions are very often made without the support and consensus of the people.
During political rallies, politicians are on the stage, which is at a higher level than the rest of the people. Politicians seldom pose questions to the people. Their speeches are usually one-sided monologues, telling people how problems can be solved.

In these one-way, linear, top-to-bottom dynamics, the majority of people are passive pupils, literally behaving like small and dependent children, who have handed over the responsible role to the politicians. Often, people expect politicians to take full responsibility for the people's lives, which were given to the politicians during the elections.

In return, citizens are expected to be obedient, pay state taxes, and often to stand by and implement politicians' decisions, which the citizens haven't even been asked about. The greatest power that the people have is periodical, once in 4-5 years (in democracies) during the elections, when a new President, Prime Minister or leadership team needs to be chosen.

This conventional transfer of responsibility, and the projection of power from many individuals (people/employees) to one or several persons (government/management team), in today's terms of co-creativity, is simply unrealistic and excessive, and only feeds the narcissistic beliefs behind the autocratic myth of "one leader, the special one, the leader saviour".

At the heart of the above dynamics lie unconscious fears and behaviors, like control, self-interest, punishment, blame, manipulation, etc. Surrounded by these fearsome psychological conditions, the usual reaction of our mind and body is to be tensed; and when these components are in the mix, at the personal or systemic level, the subject is in survival mode and his/her creativity, innovation and performance always go down.

The dynamics described above, which begin in the family, continue in the classroom, and still function in many organizations and in the political world, have served humanity (some people more than others) in the last centuries. Thankfully, according to many thought leaders, these dynamics are nearing the completion of their usefulness and functionality.
More and more frequently, we are faced with the fact that these old conventional methodologies do not work as they should, and are harmful to the individual, to organizations, and to humanity at large.
Margaret Wheatley, one of the most influential organizational thinkers of our time, calls this old system the "definition of insanity", and the time that will replace this system "a new era of healthy mind"[16].

The era that is in front of humanity, and the challenges that it brings, are

---

[16] "Finding Our Way" Margaret J. Wheatley, Barrett-Koehler 2005

impossible to solve with the outdated tools and methods that we have used before. Environmental issues, global warming, the lack of food and clean water, the turbulent economic market, and the growing difference between the rich and poor are just some of the facts and indicators that humanity, more than ever before, is in need of modern, **post conventional** values and ways in which we can manage and lead people, institutions and nations.

We need a new value system that will function and be equally useful for all. We need new tools and methodologies for empowering, managing and communicating with people and institutions. A new kind of intelligence and consciousness, a new kind of collective responsibility and leadership.

Similar to the other democracies, and in reflection of the global trends, corporation Macedonia is part of this global definition of madness.
Like never ever before, the corporation Macedonia is at present, and has been for the past two decades, an environment where, under the guise of democracy and in the name of the "salvation of the people", the leadership structures practice a form of corrupt pseudo-democracy; where there is all for a few chosen people, and very little for everyone else. This Macedonian madness dominates and is most obvious in the criminal privatization of the state assets in the nineties, the pollution of Skopje air, the enormous politicized public administration, the growing indebtedness of the state and municipalities, as well as the growing tension and hate among young people of different ethnicities and political parties.

* * *

I see this madness as a form of "Pavlovian" reflex, in a social context. This is what we have learned and what we know, this is our "comfort zone". To be liberated – to break through this dysfunctional way of knowing and existing, we need to re-invent and co-create our systems.

1. Systemic leadership – "Co-Creation"

Besides technology, co-creation must be the second largest driver of our future.

Mary-Ann Schreurs
Dutch Design Week 2013

If the global problems and economic challenges are dealt with in the old-fashioned way, without the inclusion and the support of the wider system, if the political and economic leaders continue to act alone, we simply don't stand a chance of making the shift needed to take our organizations, communities, nations and the whole planet to a new level of existence (locally and/or globally). Without a whole-system approach, the strategies for development will continue to collapse, or in the best case, they will give the average results that we already know, results that nobody wants, that support only a few of us and only in the short term.

Fortunately, the evolution of human consciousness is developing and is showing us that the old and dysfunctional "leadership" methods are aging, and new **post conventional** leadership models are needed and are emerging on the stage. One such model is the **systemic leadership model**[17].

Systemic leadership sees the organization (system) as a living being, created by many living beings (employees, or citizens in the context of society) interacting amongst themselves. In a larger context, organizations interact with other organizations, nations with other nations. All of us – people, organizations and nations – interact with the largest system of all, nature and the planet. The intent of systemic leadership is to bring each person (employee-citizen) into balanced alignment with the rest of the people in the system (organization-community). The departments in alignment with other departments in the organization, and the organization in alignment with other organizations, and so on, as far as bringing nations in alignment with other nations on the planet – in cohesive, balanced, sustainable, and healthy **ECO** units that care about the well-being of all, including oneself[18].

---

[17] The Fifth Discipline: The Art and Practice of the Learning Organization, Peter Senge, Currency 1990
[18] Leading from the emerging future, Otto Scharmer & Katrin Kaufer 2013 Barrett and Koehler

This leadership model, and the leaders who practice it, replace fear with trust and empowerment, replace command and control with support and cooperation.

A key goal of systemic leadership is to achieve a natural state of relaxation and alignment among the members of the system, and to align the system with the greater "ECO" whole.

Under such conditions, the body and the mind of the individual, as well as the system itself, often reach their natural state of being, energy, and flow[19]. In this state, the person and/or the system is highly creative and innovative, and is also in balance with the environment. The performances are at the highest possible level.

This natural state is impossible to achieve when functioning from the "EGO" positions of chronic tension, stress, frustration and fear (the main current features of corporation Macedonia, and many other global organizations and systems).

This natural process, and a state in which a living being (a person or a system) strives to actualize itself and becomes one with the whole, has been called entelechy, first by Aristotle and in recent times by the biologist Rupert Sheldrake. It is my belief that one of the key new leadership skills and roles of the post conventional leader is to understand this unstoppable natural dynamic, to recognize its patterns, and to develop platforms for supporting its unfolding. The efforts to control or suppress this movement are counter-productive, inefficient, against evolution, and are in a sense counter-leadership.

This condition of flow in the organization is reflected by the reduced entropy in the system, and the increased alignment among its members. This is not an idealized or impossible state. This is a natural condition that humankind and our modern fast-paced civilization have somehow forgotten.

The organizations that practice this style of leadership develop a culture of creativity and innovation, and function balanced on all the seven levels of consciousness (the seven "cylinders"). They equally value the seven levels of

---

[19] Csikszentmihalyi, Mihaly (1990). *Flow: The Psychology of Optimal Experience*. New York: Harper and Row

organizational functioning, by valuing profit and their employees' health (level 1), maintaining open communication within and outside the organization (level 2), focusing on productivity and excellence (level 3), being innovative (level 4), being creative (level 5), caring for the environment (level 6), and being leaders who care for future generations (level 7).

Among the many authors dealing with the phenomenon of exceptional performance in organizations and systems that are using the systemic approach, is James Surowiecki. In his book "The wisdom of crowds"[20], he says:
"Our collective intelligence is often superior to the intelligence of the smartest individual in the group."
This is also shown in the experience of Ronald A. Hejfetz and Donald L. Laurebo, described in their article titled "The Work of Leadership" published in 1997 in the Harvard Business Review[21].

The experiences of many companies who practice and use systemic leadership methodologies and tools confirm this conclusion, and show results that are not only sustainable, but also superior in comparison to others.

Collective intelligence

The most important thing that will move humanity forward, is to break down the boundaries between people and to function as a single intelligence.

David Bohm[22]

Suroviecki gives dozens of examples of extraordinary reality, in confirmation of the fact that collective intelligence is superior in comparison to the intelligence of an individual leader, regardless of his/her experience, education, or position in the company. He writes:

If you take a large group of ordinary people from different backgrounds, and you ask them to make decisions that have a common interest, the decisions of the group will be superior in comparison to the decisions of the individual leader or expert, no matter how smart s/he is or how much experience or wisdom s/he has.

---

[20] James Surowiecki "The wisdom of crowds" Anchor Books 2005
[21] http://hbr.org/2001/12/the-work-of-leadership/ar/1
[22] http://en.wikipedia.org/wiki/Bohm_Dialogue

Systemic intelligence is always smarter and wiser than the leader or the leadership team

In the case of our corporation Macedonia, we can find a confirmation that this is indeed true, if we observe the third column of the measurement (**Picture 1.11**). This column represents an intelligent systemic response in the form of recommended values, which arises from the collective intelligence of the society that best knows how to self-actualize and improve itself[23].

In the third column, we notice the new desired value of **cooperation**, which is a wise balancing counter-measure to the typical *blame* game (a limiting value in the second column) in which the two main political parties waste time and resources.
Furthermore, aware of the environmental pollution (a limiting value) of the air in Skopje, the system requires not one, but two new values and behaviors, in the form of environmental awareness and ecological awareness.
Contrary to the collective intelligence is when managers and politicians ignore the fact that the system is wiser than the individual, and bring in unilateral decisions, solutions and plans, without engaging employees and/or the ordinary citizens in the processes of thinking and decision-making. In such conditions, it is no surprise when the strategies brought in at the top are not implemented as designed.

System leaders – "Co-Creators"

The new post conventional leaders need to become systemic thinkers and doers. In a positive sense, they need to understand and to accept the limitations of their personal intelligence, in comparison with the collective intelligence.

The systemic leader needs to become an ally of the collective intelligence. S/he or they (the executive team) need to serve the system by developing co-creative platforms and interventions through which the

---

[23] Just to remind you that the third column of values is derived from the question "What values would you most like to see in your municipality-town?".

collective intelligence, wisdom and innovation will emerge, and be distilled through the co-creative process by the system itself.

Betty Sue Flouers, co-author of the book "Presence"[24], says:
The leadership of the future will not come from a particular individual – "the leader", but from groups, communities and networks.

System leaders will have to learn to overcome their fears (described in the first three levels of consciousness). They will also need to practice how to release their unrealistic power and control over the situations and people they manage; to **replace the top-to-bottom** autocratic management style with trust, support, cooperation, co-creation and wisdom. By doing this, systemic leaders simply share their responsibility with all the employees and/or the citizens in the system. System leaders need to ask important **key questions**, rather than tell and/or give orders. By doing this, they put employees/citizens on an equal level with themselves, and show the people that their opinions, energy and contributions to the system are important.

Asking important key questions allow people to think, and to be part of the collective solution. In this way, systemic leaders return the power to those who create the system. **By doing this, systemic leadership empowers the "common man"**, which in turn empowers the whole system.

Functioning in this way, the system doesn't have a single leader who will lead or save the organization or the nation, but rather a shared systemic responsibility and a systemic leadership.

"I SEE THE WHOLE SCHOOL AS A SINGLE TEACHER."

A.H. Almaas
Co-Founder of the Ridhwan School and the Diamond Approach

This systemic platform allows the ordinary citizens to continually evolve, and the organization to function as a learning system. The student, the employee, and the citizen in this way become aware of their own value and contribution to the

---

[24] "Presence" – Exploring profound change in people, organizations and society, Peter M. Senge, Joseph Jaworski, C. Otto Scharmer and Betty Sue Flowers, Nicholas Brealey publishing 2005

system – society. This co-creative dynamic empowers the people with the feelings of belonging, unity, responsible contribution, satisfaction, and meaning, and the whole system vibrates and functions at a higher frequency, becoming more creative, innovative, productive, and sustainable.

In this way, systemic leadership achieves a balanced and aligned allocation of team and/or organizational responsibilities and activities. The huge burden shifts from the shoulders of the "lone leader" or the executive leadership team (executive team, government), and is shared by everyone else in the system. This whole-system engagement is necessary in order to attain sustainability, and to tackle the big problems and challenges that today exist in reality. The ordinary citizen, from being a passive observer, becomes a systemic co-creator and a leader, who takes responsibility at his/her level, in his/her field of interest or expertise. S/he becomes an equal influencer in the system. The ordinary employee/citizen becomes a **systemic leader**[25].

**Leadership is never in an individual,
Leadership is always relational.**

This leadership style is a reality. Over 6,000 companies on the planet use the tools for measuring and managing organizational culture. Several regions and countries throughout the world have also made the first pioneering steps in applying systemic leadership nationwide.

Corporation Macedonia has taken the first real step in this direction. A values measurement like the one made in 2009 needs to be repeated once every year. Ideally, this process must be supported by the highest forms of economic, social and political leadership.
The diagnostic assessment needs to be used as a guide for the development of various strategies, creative dialogues, and leadership interventions.
In addition to the national level, these measurements need to be performed by municipalities, ministries, and in all major public companies managed by the state, mainly because they have the highest rate of entropy and outflow of energy and resources.
In fact, the measurement and the management of the organizational and national culture, as well as the promotion of systemic leadership, need to be instigated,

---

[25] http://www.youtube.com/watch?v=5JLKKy53q4s

supported and paid for by the government itself at the national level, and by the executive directors at the company level.

Additionally, it is necessary to create innovative platforms for collective thinking and action, which will mobilize and include virtually all citizens and institutions in a cohesive direction – the "**Creation of an aligned nation and institutions with an innovative culture, creativity, high performances and high standards of living.**"

These platforms will enable the emergence of the collective energy and intelligence. Through such a process, the responsibility will be shared and balanced among all stakeholders in corporation Macedonia: the students and ordinary citizens, the public sector and also private businesses, and the current political leadership as well as the opposition.

In their book "Large Group Interventions", authors Bunker and Alban [26] comment on the usefulness of such interventions, putting it simply:

People are willing to support activities for which they were asked, and influenced the decision making about them.

In order to create platforms for collective alignment and breakthrough, the next step for corporation Macedonia and its leaders [27] is the start of **creative dialogue** on issues that matter.

---

[26] Large Group Interventions: Engaging the Whole System for Rapid Change, 1997 Jossey-Bass Barbara Benedict Bunker & Billie T. Alban
[27] According to the systemic thinking, in an organization every member, regardless of his position is a systemic leader. In such circumstances, the responsibility and the action/s for change and/or transformation, does not need to come only from the top of the hierarchy, but each individual can form a creative dialogue in its environment - micro system. Note the example of the company's book of Zappos that will follow in the coming pages.

2. Creative Dialogue

"The most important work in the new economy is creating conversations."

Alan Webber

Fast Company magazine

Creative dialogue is a modern, holistic, co-creative platform for the support, development and transformation of people and organizations.
This inclusive platform is based on, and uses as a driving force, the creative power of the collective intelligence which is naturally nested within the system.

I will spare readers by not inventing a new name, and simply use the term **creative dialogue**, although this activity/intervention can also be simply named **dialogue**. Authors like Edgar H. Schein use the term "**humble inquiry**" when referring to similar processes[28]; and although it has some similarities with the appreciative inquiry (AI) process, creative dialogue is not the same as AI.

The final results of the processes of creative dialogue/inquiry are the release of creative energy, innovation, increased alignment, and a sense of flow in the system. Participants and authors who have had experience with this kind of process often describe this feeling as a **collective breakthrough**.

Today, this platform is used in education from an early age, where children in schools learn how to communicate with respect, humility and confidence with their peers in the classroom[29]. It is also successfully used to release the creative energy of young students[30].

Throughout history, one of the most interesting examples of creative dialogue is the tribal circle beside the fire, practiced by many tribes in America and Africa. Here, the life of the community would openly be discussed among the elders, women and children.

---

[28] Humble Inquiry, Edgar H Schein, Paperback 2013

[29] Creative Dialogue - Talk for Thinking in the Classroom, Robert Fishler, 2009 Routledge
[30] http://www.youtube.com/watch?v=GWAHf6BdHO0

"We talk and talk, until the talk starts."

Old American Indian saying

Nelson Mandela, in his autobiography, often referred to memories of his childhood when his village and tribe gathered together with the tribal chiefs, and talked about life and the challenges and problems in the community. The head (chief), Mandela says, was not acting as a powerful dictator, but rather as a shepherd dog. He with his presence and support, through open dialogue, guided the herd – the tribe– towards the wise future.

These forms of transformative leadership intervention, and the methodology of creative dialogue, are currently used by government agencies in many countries, as well as by leading multinational companies, in order to establish strategies for development, create new products, improve the culture, etc.

An example of such a company is **Zappos**. Zappos is a company worth several billion U.S. Dollars, which specializes in selling shoes online. Their success is based on creating an exceptional organizational culture, based on a platform that resembles the dynamics of creative dialogue.
Each year, employees from the "Zappos family" write open essays about what Zappos means for them, about the Zappos values and culture, and the meaning of the organization. These essays are then collected and published in the annual "Zappos Culture Book"[31].
The end result: Zappos is a company with a tremendous organizational culture and excellent results, and is a desired place to work.
People at Zappos often say:

"All employees are leaders at Zappos."

Pioneering and innovative steps to enhance the values and culture have also been taken at the national level. Creative dialogues have been run in Australia and South Africa. Perhaps the most significant large group intervention activity of this kind has been used in Iceland[32] in 2009, based upon which the new national vision and strategy have been developed for the country, following the banking

---

[31] http://www.youtube.com/watch?v=H06kDgRjEgg
[32] http://www.youtube.com/watch?v=i_YF0IrJ4dM

crisis. (Icelandic banks were the first to collapse in 2007, which signaled the big crisis that followed in 2007-2008.)

Corporation Macedonia, like many other organizations, today and in the past 20 years, has been functioning contrary to the co-creative principles of systemic leadership and creative dialogue. It is generally governed by top-to-bottom, linear, conventional, autocratic leaders who, under the coat of democracy and mutual blame, keep their people in chronic tension, fear, and frustration. These fear-based conditions are counter-productive, since they do not create safe "containers" and conditions for the release of the creative potential (physical, emotional, mental, and spiritual) of the people of Macedonia.

This outdated, conventional, "good but not great" leadership style in corporation Macedonia, which is often seen throughout the world, needs to be transformed and re-invented, from being linear and autocratic to being systemic and co-creational.

This transformation of culture at the national level needs to be driven by the transformation of the leaders and their consciousness. Until that happens, the corporation Macedonia will remain a mediocre, tense and frustrated community, which will be abandoned by its most talented young people and lose their energy.

Creative dialogue is not the same as the dialogue we know

MIT professor and a world leader in this field, William (Bill) Isaacs, in his book "Dialogue - the art of thinking together"[33] says:

"Dialogue is a conversation with a center."

According to him, in order to design and lead a dialogue that will create **collective insights** and **breakthroughs**, we need to create so-called **containers** (safe conditions) where the people in the system, and the system as a whole, can and will relax and enter the natural flow. Then, out of this pool of collective wisdom, creativity and innovation will emerge and transform the people and the system. New strategies are born, new products and services emerge, and new co-creative relationships are formed.

---

[33] "Dialogue and the Art of Thinking Together"- A Pioneering Approach to Communicating in Business and in Life, William Isaacs, Doubleday 1999

Isaacs states that to develop the conditions for achieving this flow, the system needs to develop four key practices:

1) Active listening
2) Respecting one another and the difference of opinions
3) Stopping (suspending) judgments and the culture of blame
4) Expressing our own voice

In this context, according to Isaacs, leadership is the capacity to create and maintain a container of safety, support and cooperation, in which there is a room for a lot of different transformational ideas.

This container presents a safety zone in which various pressures and crises can occur during the dialogue, and can metabolize and transform through the prolonged withstanding of the creative tensions.
From this point of view, leadership creates containers that support major cultural transformations.
The collective breakthrough, liberated creativity, and innovation emerge as a result of the shared experience of the relaxed system that has entered the natural state of flow – oneness.

When I use the word "**creative dialogue**" I need to make a very precise distinction between the creative dialogue that will be described in the following pages, and the dialogues and debates that dominate in our classrooms, schools, workplaces, and the parliaments of many democracies. Although in all these institutions there is a dialogue, which sometimes could be creative, it is usually dominated by the awareness, values and language – **the monologue** – of the professor, the boss, the director or the politician. In these cases, there is no equal involvement of others in the dialogue. **The flow of collective intelligence and energy can't be accessed**, and therefore the creativity and the innovation of the system are put on stand-by.

The monologue kills collective intelligence, creativity and innovation from the first moment.

In parliaments, the openness is limited in the basic framework of the parliament. The same situation occurs in the offices of managers or directors. In boardrooms, the openness is limited by the decisions of the directors, and their control, awareness and responsibility remain confined to their circle. Even here, they don't listen with equality, and not everyone is included.

From this position in which the wider system is turned off, there is neither access to nor impact from the collective intelligence. In situations like this, there is no co-creation.

The dominant form of debates works similarly. Here, two or more sides compete for the best position, vying to establish who is smarter, better and stronger.

	Ego functioning	Eco functioning
Who is included?	Me, I or "We" as a particular group of "special ones". The others are excluded.	"We" as a whole ECO unit.
Communication style	Linear. One person or an "important few" dominate space and time. Command and control. Debate, monologue.	Systemic. Co-creation, in which the whole system participates. Creative dialogue.
Energy in the container	Fear, anxiety, lack of support, blame, attack, not safe to voice differences. System is tensed, and breakthrough and flow is impossible.	Support, allowing differences, safety, presence. System relaxes with time, and breakthrough and flow naturally emerge.

With this kind of dialogue/debate, there are several problems. The decisions are simply made in a linear, top-down fashion, which makes their implementation difficult from the very beginning. The executive team or the government makes a decision regarding an issue, which needs to be implemented through a particular strategy. However, the ordinary employee or the citizen who is expected to implement this strategy is often unfamiliar with and/or excluded from the process of thinking and decision-making behind the strategy. These people are often manipulated, ignored and underestimated with regard to decisions that directly affect them. No wonder so many people, not only in Macedonia but all around the world, are apathetic and disinterested in their place and role in society and/or their contribution at work.

In this way it is very difficult, if not impossible, to ask for engagement or responsibility from someone who has not directly participated in the dialogue or in the decision-making.
The end result is the system functioning with a mediocre performance and a minimal use of its potential.

Modern Methods and Tools

Unlike the old, outdated, largely autocratic and obviously dysfunctional management methods and tools, there are several modern methods which are used as platforms for creative dialogue.
The key difference of these tools and methods, when compared with the linear monologue, is that they create a space for equality and the inclusion of all stakeholders in the system, thus allowing the **collective intelligence to emerge and unfold**. These models are **systemic** and **co-creative**. Using this type of management, the knowledge, wisdom and intelligence of the individualistic boss, director or president is many times surpassed by the collective intelligence of the system.

I want to mention that my research is not focused on how these systemic methodologies modify and/or question the hierarchical functioning of the system that uses them. My core purpose is to show how they can serve organizations and nations, as platforms for finding new creative and innovative ideas and for developing knowledge and strategies that work.

I will mention a few of these tools and methodologies that I have encountered, which have been used in past decades:
From the older generation, before and up to the nineties: Search Conference, Future Search, Real Time Strategic Change, Real Time Work Design, Participative Design, Simu-Real, Work-Out, Large Scale Interactive Events, and Open Space Technology[34].
Since the nineties, and until the first decade of the 21st century: Appreciative Inquiry and the World Café.

---

[34] Large Group Interventions: Engaging the Whole System for Rapid Change, 1997 Jossey-Bass, Barbara Benedict Bunker & Billie T. Alban

And the latest methodologies, which are actually sophisticated distillates of all the previous ones, are: the dialogic interventions of Isaacs, Scharmer's "U Theory", and the breakthrough methodologies of the consultancy NOWHERE.

The above methodologies, especially the post-nineties ones, do not affect the system in just a linear way; they are multi-dimensional, and in my experience, they represent the latest leadership models for optimizing the functioning and efficiency of teams and organizations.

A common feature of these methods is that when they are used in the organizational context, they create teams with a high degree of alignment, creativity, innovation, and performance.

What makes creative dialogue innovative and inspirational?

Nick Udal, the founder and a CEO of the consultancy NOWHERE, who is also chair of the Global Agenda Council on New Models of Leadership at the World Economic Forum, has dedicated his latest book to the new leadership skills needed to master, deliver, and ride a "**creative rollercoaster**"[35] - this is how Nick and his crew at NOWHERE refer to the creative dialogues and deep dives interventions.

His description of the rollercoaster overlaps with the findings and experiences of both Isaacs with his dialogues, and Otto Scharmer in his U Theory.

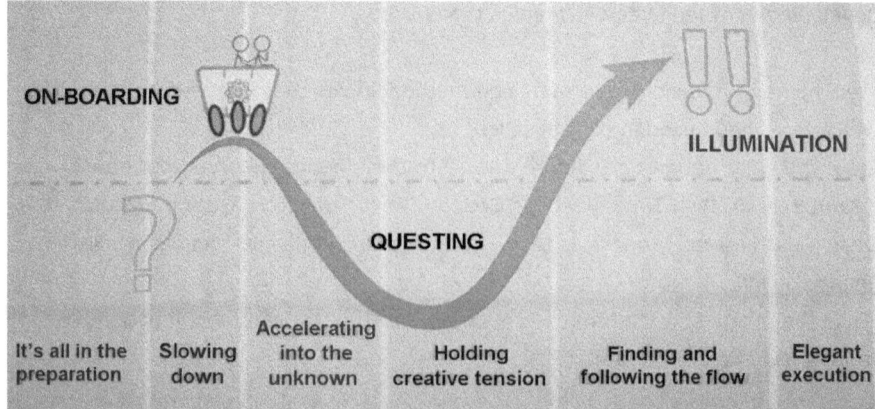

Picture 2.2: The creative rollercoaster experience. Picture taken from Nick Udal's

---

[35] Riding the creative rollercoaster, Nick Udal, Kogan Page 2014

book, "Riding the creative rollercoaster"

I will use the above illustration from Udal's book to describe what happens in the processes of creative dialogue/inquiry:

The building of the container starts at the beginning of the intervention. Great attention is paid to the quality of the space where the intervention takes place. High levels of natural daylight and a wide open space makes a huge difference. The quality of the contact between the participants in the dialogue is paramount, since this is what makes the container safe, supportive and trustful. Participants are seated in a circle, or sets of circles.
To begin the creative dialogue, it is necessary to have a key question – the **Breakthrough Question**, as Udal calls it.
The key question is necessary primarily as a kind of focused elastic which continuously maintains the creative tension. The key question, together with the build-up of the container, serves as a kind of coach or car, in which all the stakeholders embark together and begin the process of diving into the unknown. This is the subtle phase of preparation – **on-boarding**.

The stable formation of the container is the responsibility of the leader or leadership team. This is usually done with the help of an experienced catalyst – a person who has a high capacity for maintaining presence, as well as for holding the creative tension that occurs within the system during the dialogue, especially while the team is in the zone of the unknown/**questing**.
Holding the creative tension during this period is crucial. This zone is dominated by very difficult feelings to sit with, such as impatience, fear, frustration, inadequacy, helplessness, anger, etc. Most people faced with these feelings are reactive and impulsive, and reject them, thus not allowing what is present to be there. Navigating through this zone is a real rollercoaster, which requires high levels of skill and the will to withstand this pressure. It is only after holding this storm long enough, that the system reaches the level of relaxation (the moment of breakthrough), and enters the creative flow – **Illumination**.

If in any way the system ignores and suppresses this tense energy (due to the reactivity caused by impatience, or the desire to take impulsive action), or avoids it (because it is an uncomfortable feeling), or in case the catalyst simply cannot hold the tension, the process simply collapses, and the system continues to operate in the zone of comfort (flat line) that gives the same old known performance.

Similarly to Udal's description, Bill Isaacs describes four communicational stages through which the group passes, from the beginning of the dialogue (the key question position) all the way to the breakthrough/illumination (**Picture 2.3**):

1. Politeness - Shared monologues
2. Breakdown - Debate
3. Inquiry – Reflective dialogue
4. Flow – Generative dialogue

We could say that the first two stages have a competitive, Ego-based background, while the third and the fourth stages are rooted in the holistic/systemic/co-creative Eco approach.

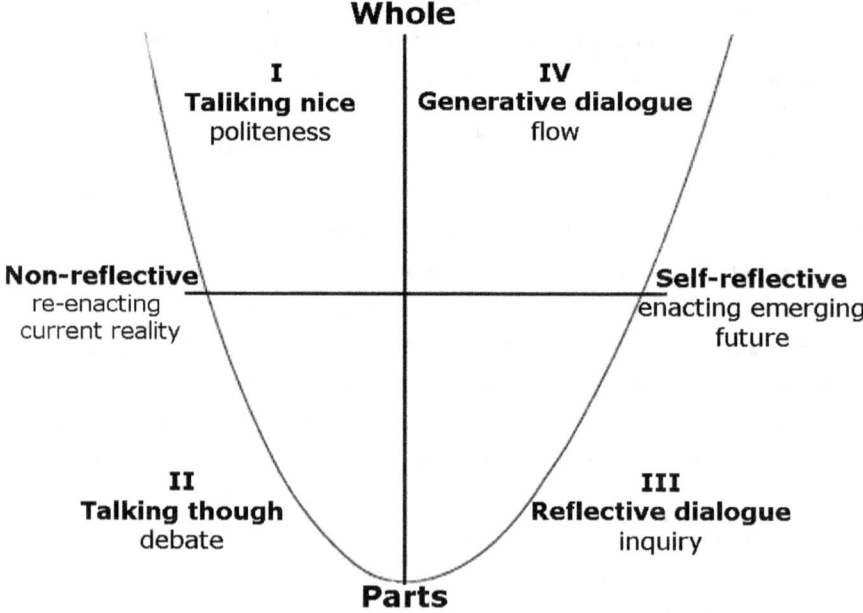

Picture 2.3: Diagram of communicational stages, from Isaacs' book "Dialogue and the art of thinking together"

Isaacs' and Udal's experiences and realizations are almost identical to what Otto Scharmer describes in his "U Theory"[36].

Otto Scharmer is a global leader in the field of new social and transformative leadership technologies. His 10 years of research at the MIT in this domain have materialized in his book "Theory U", which is a comprehensive and detailed description of what actually happens during the process of creative dialogues. His analysis can actually be used as a microscopic (step by step) illustration of the process of creative dialogue/inquiry.

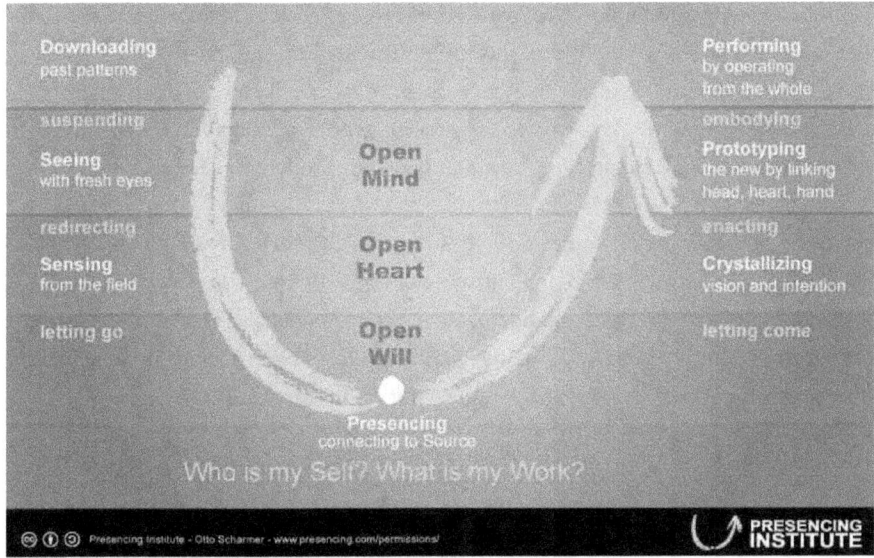

Picture 2.4: taken from the Presencing INSTITUTE

Scharmer identifies 7 key stages of this transformative process.

1. Downloading – Re-enacting patterns of the past, repeating old habits and knowledge, through familiar thought patterns.

2. Seeing – Suspending judgment and looking at reality with fresh eyes – the observed system is separate from those who observe.

3. Sensing – Connecting to the field and attending to the situation from the whole – the boundary between observer and observed collapses, the system begins to see itself.

4. Presencing – Connecting with the deepest source, from which the field of the future begins to arise – viewing from the source.

5. Crystallizing vision and intention – Envisioning the new future that wants to emerge.

---

[36] "Theory U" – leading from the future as it emerges, C. Otto Scharmer, Barrett-Koehler 2009

6. Prototyping – Living microcosms in order to explore the future by doing, enacting the new, through "being in dialogue with the universe".

7. Performing – Embodying the new, in practices and infrastructures – embedding the new in the context of the larger co-evolving ecosystem.

Several ideas overlap between the dialogic methodologies of Isaacs, the U Theory of Scharmer, and the catalytic interventions of the NOWHERE consultants. They all propose **dialogue** as powerful catalyst of the systemic transformation, and they all suggest skillful and willful diving into the **unknown**.

All these methods, for which I use the words creative dialogue, are applicable to any process of learning, knowledge transference, and/or transformation, including consulting, coaching, mentoring, strategy building, product development, etc.

The problem that many of us face, including business leaders, institutions, and humanity at large, is that too often in the process of learning, we use the familiar knowledge from our comfort zone (**downloading**). This is why individuals and organizations flat-line, time and again. When downloading, the depth of learning and knowledge management remains superficial, thereby reducing the likelihood of any future creativity, innovation, and performances to naturally unfold.

"U Theory", creative dialogue and corporation Macedonia

If you look at companies in light of what they could be, however, most commercial corporations are underachievers. They exist at an early stage of evolution; they develop and exploit only a small fraction of their potential.

Arie de Geus "The Living Company"[37]

If for a moment we take as an example the key challenge with which corporation Macedonia is faced, which is the high unemployment rate, and we look at it in the context of a key strategic question, to which we need to find an innovative and inspiring solution:

How do we create 300,000 new jobs?

---

[37] http://hbr.org/1997/03/the-living-company/ar/

If we approach this issue by **downloading** (an approach that to date has been primary in decision-making in corporation Macedonia), then the results will be average, as in the actual reality in Macedonia.
This problem of unemployment has been ongoing for the past 20 years, and it has not been resolved; nor have any serious results that differ in any way been produced during this period.

What I am suggesting is that for such a key issue, we in Macedonia (and we on the planet) need to approach the question in a **co-creative** way, such as the **creative dialogue**, using **U Theory** or some form of **systemic inquiry** that will lead us to a **collective breakthrough**. The experiences of organizations that have worked and are working using such methods show collective breakthroughs, increased innovations, greater creativity, and higher energy within the system, as well as highly improved results and internal relationships, compared to when people use the old methods of **downloading**.

Corporation Macedonia needs the "U Theory", in reality and symbolically. In English slang, the term "U-turn" is used when someone needs to take a direction totally opposite to the one they are currently on.
Leaders of corporation Macedonia (similar to many world leaders) use unproductive and unsustainable Ego-based methods of downloading, which do not support the creation of the safety containers that are needed for transformation and liberation of the creative and innovative energies of organizations and society.
The two main political parties, the nationalist (conservatives) and the social-democrats, constantly blame each other for national problems, in a ping-pong manner. There is no creative dialogue between them or within the system. The end results are unproductive for the whole system.

This leadership style is reactive, based on fear, intimidation and control.
It is because of this situation that corporation Macedonia needs a serious "U-turn".
With such outdated leadership methods, corporation Macedonia will not be able to solve the challenges and the problems it faces in the 21st century; and if we continue in the same direction, we will reach a dead-end, where the chances of attaining the desired economic growth and improved standards of living are

minimal. I believe this is as true for Macedonia as for many other organizations and nations in the world.

You cannot solve problems with the same way of thinking in which they were created.

Albert Einstein

In my experience, despite the high entropy and the misaligned culture which doesn't support our development strategies, corporation Macedonia suffers from a lack of systemic leaders who use co-creative platforms to build containers that can support the creative tensions and collective breakthroughs. In fact, this use of co-creation may be the biggest challenge for leaders in Macedonia and in general.

Key questions for creative dialogue

"It's the question that drives us, Neo..."

Trinity to Neo, in the movie "The Matrix"

Good companies work with answers, excellent companies work with questions. If you ask the organization the right question, that is more powerful than the answers they already have.
Nick Udal - NOWHERE

During the practice of the creative dialogue, several things need to be kept in mind:
- The inclusion of everyone in the system
- The creation of key questions
- The practice and maintenance of presence

The inclusion of each participant in the dialogue is achieved by granting an equal amount of time and an equal opportunity for expression to each participant (without exception). In a conversation I had with Matt Clark, an experienced catalyst and one of the directors of the NOWHERE consulting firm, he told me:

"In the creative dialogue, there is no room for observers."

I would add to this that in the creative dialogue, there is no place for monologues.

Because of this, one of the instructions given to the circle of participants in the creative dialogue, is to be aware and avoid falling into the trap of their own monologue, in which they would take up too much space and time. The opposite is also important, when people are not speaking and contributing at all.
In the first case, people who talk too much in the circle are required to balance and reduce their monologues. In the latter case, those who participate less are encouraged to voice their opinions and balance their place in the system, despite any feelings of shame, the fear of mistakes, or the fear of being judged.

The second goal, after the inclusion of all participants, is the creation of key questions which have meaning and importance to the team and/or organization at a given moment.

Questions, as powerful tools for learning and development, have been used for centuries by wise teachers. Socrates was famous for his teaching methodology, based on good questions. He is known to have said: **I cannot teach anybody anything, I can only make them think.**

Similarly to Socrates, one of the greatest minds and thinkers of the 20th century, Einstein, said: **"The key thing is to not stop asking questions. If I have an hour to solve the problem on which my life depends, I would devote the first 55 minutes to asking the right question, because if I have a real question, I will solve the problem in less than five minutes".**

This book itself is the result of the creative tension that arose while maintaining several key questions:
How do we transform and innovate the Macedonian culture, and our organizations and institutions?
How do we improve the quality of life of our citizens?
What kind of leadership do we need to do this?

Contemporary psychology, especially modern coaching, pays great attention to the questions it asks.

The coach is a careful creator of well-formed questions, whose primary objective is to create awareness and responsibility in the coachee or the coached team. John Whitmore[38], one of the fathers of modern coaching, says that coaching is actually creating awareness and responsibility in people and organizations; and the manager or coach, in the process of managing people, needs to be focused on creating these two qualities in them, which is done by asking key questions. Many coaches say that the manager who coaches by asking questions, and in this way includes and empowers people, turns from a manager into a leader.

Let me give an interesting illustration that describes the impact of questions in the processes of thinking and answering.

Think of a glowing object that freely falls from the dark sky – such as a lighting parachute slowly descending, attracted by the Earth's gravity, and illuminating the space around it. Or shining fluorescent sticks, thrown into a deep, dark vertical well.

In the same way as the shining parachute or fluorescent sticks, questions have the effect of being **illuminators of the consciousness**, expanding our comfort zone and stimulating an increased awareness in the processes of dialogue/inquiry.

This is particularly true when we **hold the question** and allow the tension to work on us, rather than attempt to answer it straight away.

At a group level, during the creative dialogue/inquiry, the effect of a powerful question on which the whole group is focused is multiplied; and the illumination of consciousness at a particular point happens throughout the system, affecting and touching all the participants involved. This is the moment of breakthrough (passing the threshold, entering the flow...). **It is at this point of collective illumination that the group starts to think together as a whole.** This is the place of unlimited creativity and innovation. **"It is here that the system surfs on the wise winds of gods"**. This effect was known to our ancestors and tribal leaders in America, or in the village in which Nelson Mandela grew up as a child. That is why it is important to carefully craft and select the key question. It must not be imposed, manipulated, or randomly selected by the executives or politicians.

---

[38] Coaching for performances John Whitmore Nicholas Bradley 1996

The key question needs to be "held" in the collective field, without being answered with rushed responses and/or activities.

Similar to the **koan**[39] practice in Zen Buddhism, the key question maintains the creative tension, and feeds the mind with curiosity.

The difference between holding a question, and answering it quickly and reactively, is huge. If you answer the question, the creative tension will be gone, and the mind will cease to "quest" and be curious. Answering the question in a fast manner and taking immediate action is often the logical choice for managers; however, this conventional attitude leads to fire-fighting and repeating what we already know, which at the end gives the same old flat-lining results.

In their book "The way of nowhere – 8 questions to release the creative potential"[40], Nick Turner and Nick Udal use eight breakthrough questions (as they call them), to release the creative potential in individuals and organizations.

1 What is my (our, for organizations) unique purpose...?
2 How am I (we) releasing the magic of the moment...?
3 How am I (we) venturing into uncertainty...?
4 How am I (we) focusing the power of my intent...?
5 How am I (we) supporting growth...?
6 How am I (we) learning to see the invisible...?
7 How am I (we) returning my/our gift...?
8 How am I (we) keeping my/our energy clean and bright?

According to them, the key question has the power to unlock the potential in people, and has the following four characteristics:

Four characteristics of the breakthrough question

1) We do not know the answer.
2) Alone, you can't find the answer. For that, we need the co-creative power and intelligence of the group.
3) The question keeps you awake at night – it maintains your intent.
4) When you find the answer, you'll change everything.

---

[39] http://www.britannica.com/EBchecked/topic/320734/koan
[40] Nick Udall & Nic Turner "The way of nowhere – 8 questions to release my/our creative potential Harper Collins 2008

Using the model of the seven levels of consciousness and the principles of creative dialogue, I have designed a question list that I simply call 7, which you can use as a platform for creating creative dialogue, and building a culture of alignment and innovation in your organization.

7 SEVEN

			Key Questions for organizations
SERVICE to HUMANITY		7	What is our purpose as organizations? Why do we exist as company? How are we serving the humanity?
MAKING a DIFFERENCE COLLABORATION WITH CUSTOMERS AND LOCAL COMMUNITY		6	How are we creating strategic alliances and partnerships? How are we creating fulfilled employees? How are we engaging with the local community to protect the environment?
INTERNAL COHESION DEVELOPMENT OF CORPORATE COMUNITY		5	How are we creating organizational alignment? How are we liberating creativity and passion in the organization? How are we uniting behind our purpose?
TRANSFORMATION CONTINUOUS RENEWAL		4	How are we learning and innovating continuously? How are we constantly sharing knowledge? How are we supporting life long learning?
SELF- ESTEEM BEING THE BEST, BEST PRACTICE		3	How are we building excellence and quality in products, systems services and processes? How do we reduce bureaucracy, hierarchy, silo - mentality, power and status seeking, confusion and arrogance?
RELATIONSHIPS THAT SUPPORT CORPORATE NEEDS		2	How are we maximizing internal as well as external communication? How are we reducing internal competition, manipulation, blame, internal politics, gender and ethnic discrimination?
SURVIVAL PURSUIT OF PROFIT & SHAREHOLDER VALUE		1	How are we creating profit and financial stability? How are we caring for the health, safety and welfare of employees? How do we reduce excessive control and caution, short term focus, corruption, greed and exploitation?

Picture 2.5: Seven key questions for organizations

In the ideal case, such as with Macedonia, were we have the diagnostics and a clear picture of the current and the desired culture, the key questions are on the surface, and all we need to do is use them as platforms for the creative dialogues.

Bad dialogue is only the dialogue that we don't have.

Leading a creative dialogue and catalyzing the change of a group/system from a blurred, stuck or comfort zone situation, to a place of breakthrough, innovation and flow, requires a high level of skill, a great deal of practice with the process, and a level of psychological maturity.
For those who are interested and willing to experiment, let's take an experimental step and see how this truly works.

I offer an exercise that you can practice and use in your team, organization or community[41]:

Let's suppose that your team has eight members, and due to certain reasons, the team has some level of dissatisfaction with its functioning, or simply wants to create something new (a project, service, or strategy).

You may split the larger system into smaller groups – in this case, you can divide the team into two smaller units of four members each.
Remember the three key things for creative dialogue:
1) Equal time for everyone to contribute
2) A key question
3) Practicing presence.

1) Choose a space with lots of daylight, clear air, and a spacious feeling. I recommend never doing this kind of work in a basement or in a room with only artificial light.

Sit with your teammates in an ideal circle, preferably without a round table in the middle. The table has the effect of being a mental and physical barrier. Keep the distance of an arm's length between you. Keep a clock handy for timing.

Determine the time interval that each of you will have in talking/answering the key question/questions.
At the beginning (this applies to small groups of two to four members), I recommend that you use shorter intervals of 5-7 minutes per person. Over time, increase your time intervals. The ideal interval for a four-member team is 10-15 minutes per person, or 40-60 minutes for a unit of four people.

2) Select a key question. At the beginning it is quite fine if you experiment with several questions. Feeling the group energy in the circle when you are considering a certain question, follow the collective energy and choose the question that has the most charge for all of you.

---

[41] Working with dialogic methodologies requires a high level of presence, and coaching and catalytic skills. Although you can learn much through practice and trial and error, to beginners in these processes, I still recommend you do this with an experienced catalyst.

With the key question, there are no compromises. It must keep you energized and awake, and hold your attention. If there is not enough energy in the question, simply do not start until you feel right.

The creation of the key question often takes time. It might take you several months of experimenting and holding several questions, until you feel that you have the right one. You may use the questions from the 7 list, to give you some ideas.

Let's imagine that the key question for your team at the moment is:
How are we creating a team that is innovative and inspirational?

You might experiment and see what works for you by trying these sub-questions:
How are we improving our functioning?
How will our team look when innovation and creativity are liberated? [42]
... etc.

When you have completed this preparation stage (called **on-boarding** by Udal), begin the creative dialogue.

VERY IMPORTANT! When one of you begins to talk, the others need to listen without interruption, comments or questions, until the speaker finishes their speech.
There will be moments when the speaker will have no answer, and a silent period will occur in the circle. Stay present in these moments and notice the silence and what is happening inside of you as a reaction to the questions and the answers that you hear. The moments of silence are useful as a support for the speaker, as well as for the whole group, as recognition that **not knowing** is also fine. These moments are referred to by Isaac and Scharmer as **"suspending"**.

Once everyone in your team completes their time, you can, as a group, discuss the experience together.

Maintain a balance between listening and talking. Suspend the judgmental voices, and stay present in your body. If you notice that the group is entering judgmental

---

[42] Be creative with the questions. You might have noticed that I often start the questions with **How are we**, and the question is in a present tense. This is not by chance. This type of question makes you look at things as if you were already doing them.

waters, or someone is dominating the group with a monologue, take a moment to remind yourself of the body and the **practice of presence**.
Shift from listening to your head (your internal dialogue and the inner critic/super ego) to listening to your body and to the whole field in the system. This may sound simple to write or read, but in reality this shift of inner listening and awareness takes lots of practice and time.

Group dialogues aim to **co-create** new knowledge, so if someone dominates with a monologue or blame, or competes over who has the smarter solution, know that you are back in the comfort zone – you are downloading old patterns, and are unlikely to have a breakthrough and create an innovative solution. Come back to presence.

Slow down, to speed up

3) **The level of presence is very important; it is paramount.**

In the zone of the unknown (questing), emotions and feelings tend to be extremely difficult and unpleasant. The feelings of not-knowing, confusion, impatience, fear, panic, anger, etc. are very difficult to sustain and endure, until they metabolize and transform. These are the most challenging moments for a team that works with creative dialogue – to withstand the pressure of this creative tension.
It is at this critical point of high tension and discomfort that most teams make the mistake of premature action-taking, which only pushes the system to exit the creative dialogue and go back to the known comfort zone – since this is the safest place. In these times, again direct your personal attention back to your body, and sense it fully, over and over again[43].

These are the moments where the role of a present catalyst is essential. S/he or they are those who hold the presence, as well as instruct the group to stay in presence. I would suggest that whenever it is possible, a group of 10-25 people needs at least two catalysts to hold the presence.

---

[43] See the exercise on p. 121 and the practice of sensing.

This process will inevitably move lots of personal emotion, as a result of what you as an individual and the whole group are going through.

During the creative dialogue and especially when the tensions increase, it is very useful and important to notice, identify, and talk about your personal experience and the emotions that you feel.

Suspend your own agenda and listen to your body, and the system. Feel the whole system – how it touches you and affects you. Speak in the first person singular, in the present tense:

At the moment, I feel..., I think..., I wonder..., etc.

In case your team is larger, or you are working on several key questions, you might need several days for the creative dialogue to reach the breakthrough stage.

With larger teams, you can also work in larger circles, as the American Indians did. It is also common practice, when this is done in several smaller groups, that the members rotate among different groups for different questions, so the group is never the same. Additionally with big systems, if the space and time allows, at the start you could minimize the circles and work in several smaller groups, which address the key question simultaneously, always concluding with the big circle at the end.

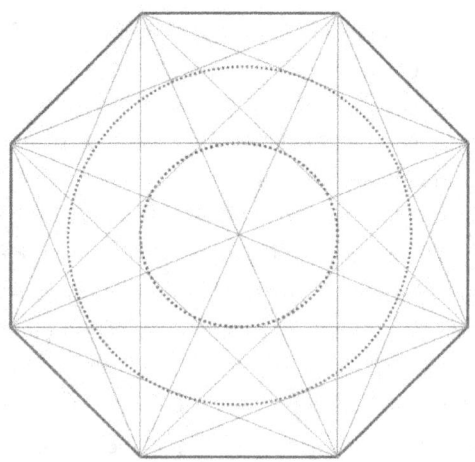

Collective illumination – breakthrough

At a certain point, in the eye of the storm, when we have sustained the creative tension for long enough, at **the bottom of the unknown (the bottom of the U)**, the boundaries collapse and the system relaxes, and reaches **"the zone"** of **flow and "knowing"** – an "aha" moment of collective breakthrough and illumination.

This knowing is very different from the everyday mode of knowing that we have while in our comfort zone – this is the **no-mind knowing**.

Through the process of creative tension and **cooking together**, we metabolize our fears and weaknesses, and reach the level of personal and collective transformation. **Sublimation of this kind is not possible in the old conventional ways of communicating and relating by downloading**, and my descriptions of it, no matter how illustrative they are, cannot explain the real experience of this moment.

As a result, the system reaches new levels of alignment, team members get to know each other on a more intimate and humane level, their confidence and mutual trust grows, and the team grows together – gaining the clarity as well as the stability and strength of a diamond.

The creativity and innovation levels reach their peak, along with the productivity, and the system emerges ready for inspirational prototyping, execution, and implementation.

Imagine, now, how powerful is the dialogic intervention in which 20, or 50, or 2,000 **co-creators** are involved[44].

At the end I still need to repeat that the processes of creative dialogue are a sophisticated leadership methodology which sometimes requires several months of preparation and dialogue, until the moment of breakthrough when the team can think together as a unit. To run such a process, leaders need to develop a high level of catalytic skills and practice. If your attempts are at the beginner's stage, do ask for support from people with experience in acting as catalysts and running creative dialogue interventions.

Key questions for corporation Macedonia

In the case of corporation Macedonia, the values measurement places it in an ideal position, since some of the key questions are already on the surface.

If we go back to the assessment, you will see what really affects corporation Macedonia (our system/team). In this context, we need to look at the measurement as a kind of expression of the collective intelligence, which only needs to be translated into key questions for the dialogic interventions that will shape the strategies and illuminate the desired path for the system.

---

[44] The methodology of Open Space has been used in groups of 2000 participants

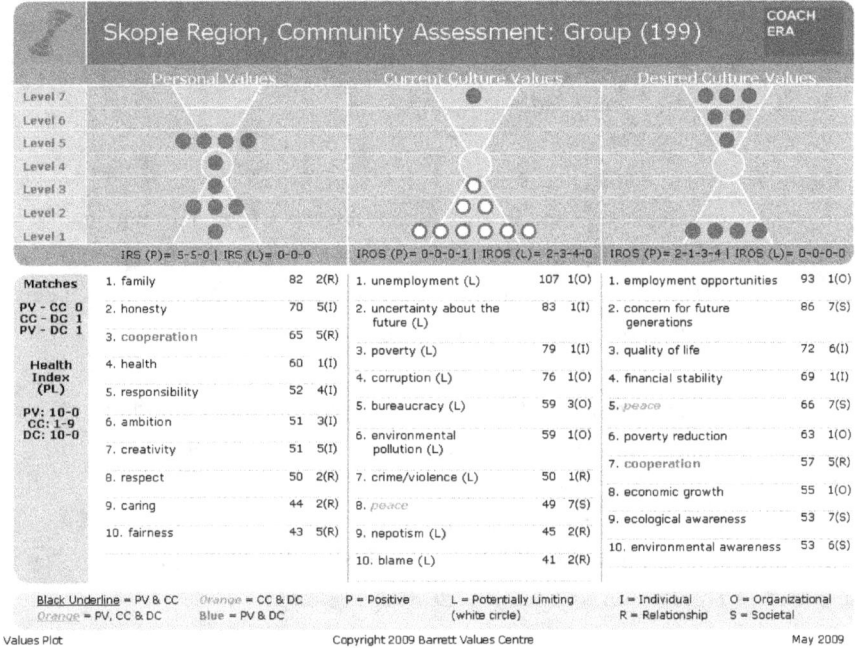

Picture 2.6: Values assessment of the Skopje region

Based on the values assessment, I have prepared a list of key questions and sub-questions that can be used for the creative dialogue. The weaknesses that come from the limiting values are converted into challenging key questions.

I offer these questions as an example and possible inspiration, but I do want to mention that those organizations that decide to use dialogic interventions need to create their own most adequate key questions, with the help of a catalyst.

Some of the questions below are of utmost importance to corporation Macedonia. Perhaps some of them are even being asked, but unfortunately there is not a proper creative dialogue around them, which will deliver a collective breakthrough and long-term innovative solutions.

These questions are considered by a small group of influential politicians and businessmen who, despite their possible good intentions, simply can't generate enough collective energy for a breakthrough and transformation, because of their isolated leadership style.

If we compare the way of functioning of the leadership structures in corporation Macedonia with the Isaacs diagram (Picture 2.3), we'll come to the conclusion that these leadership structures operate in the first two zones:

1. Polite behavior, shared monologues
2. Breakdown, controlled discussion

In these two zones, blame, accusation, tension and inefficiency dominate. These zones simply do not create enough energy to move the system into the new area of creative flow. In Otto Scharmer's terms, the leadership functions through **downloading**. These two zones do not create stable containers, and the system goes back to what it knows – the comfort zone.

On the more positive side, what brings hope is that if the current leadership structures do commit to co-creative leadership, innovation, creativity, and transformation, not just in Macedonia, but worldwide, then the dialogic interventions today are available and can be mounted in very short time periods. **These methods can bring explosions of creativity and transformation in corporation Macedonia and wherever they are used.**

The ideal scenario is these interventions being started and supported by the initiative of the top leadership team. However, if the top leadership is inflexible and resistant towards change and the needs of the current times, there are alternatives, such as creating "grass-roots" creative teams that will willingly enter a dialogue, in order to create the base for generating a collective transformation and the release of the potential of people, organizations and communities.

Key question 1

Given that the current vision of corporation Macedonia is quite unclear at the present time, I think that one of the key questions for creative dialogue in the country should be associated with this thought: **Why are we here as nation?**

To generate the breakthrough on this and other key questions may take several months, and maybe even a few years; however, past experience (Isaacs, Scharmer, Udal) shows that once the system has gone through

the breakthrough point, the difference in the way it operates, aligns and performs is simply amazing, in comparison to where it was.

I will emphasize again, since this is crucial, that reaching a breakthrough for questions like this is only possible with the co-creation of a large and diverse group of Macedonian people.

The key question number 1 is:

What is the unique role, the purpose of existence, of the current generation of Macedonian citizens? Why are we here as nation?

This essential, core question is equivalent to the question at the point of **presencing** (see Scharmer, **Picture 2.4**): Who am I/we? What is my/our work/purpose?

Other key questions

In line with the assessment, I further offer this important question:

How are we reducing the rate of unemployment? How are we creating new jobs? How are we creating new jobs apart from attracting foreign direct investments?
The participants in the creative dialogue on this particular question need to be a diverse group, with members from the private sector, the chambers of commerce, the biggest employers in the country, the leaders from the banking sector, the universities, and the most successful entrepreneurs.

How are we minimizing **corruption?**
How will Macedonia look when we bring **corruption to a minimum?**

How are we increasing **the efficiency of the public administration?**
How are we minimizing and reducing **bureaucracy?**

How are we reducing **pollution** and **protecting the environment**? This is a key question for a creative dialogue involving the ministry of environment, ecological NGOs, schools, universities, municipalities, tourism-related private and public organizations, etc.

How are we reducing **crime and violence?** How will life in Macedonia look and feel when the **crime and violence** are at a minimal level?

How are we minimizing **nepotism** in our society? How will our public services look without the limiting behavior of **nepotism**?

How are we stopping **blame** in society at all the levels (political, ethnic, or institutional)? How will society look if we replace **blame** with **cooperation**?

How are we building and improving **cooperation** at all levels? What are the benefits of **cooperation** at the interpersonal, organizational, ethnic, regional, and national levels?

How are we caring for **future generations**? How will Macedonia look with healthy **future generations**?

How are we improving the **quality of life** at all levels? How will our life, institutions, and the whole country look if we dramatically improve the **quality of life**?

How are we improving our **finances** and how are we managing them wisely at the personal, organizational, and national level? How are we educating our people and future generations on **investing** smartly?

These are some examples of key questions that can be used for creative dialogues at the micro level (your street, neighborhood, village) and macro level (company, department, region, and city).

The key questions need to be modified according to the primary needs of the particular system, and the change we want to generate in it.

These needs could easily emerge if you ask the participants in the dialogue to hold a basic simple question:

Where/what is the real need of the system?

For example, the Macedonian capital Skopje has extremely polluted air, and so the question "How are we reducing air pollution in Skopje and creating a healthy environment in the town?" is very applicable to Skopje; but this question is not at all necessary for Berovo, a mountain town in east Macedonia surrounded by forests.
Workgroups in Berovo will therefore adjust their creative dialogue considering their development needs at the local level.

At the start of this book, I mentioned the 26 countries that have undertaken culture assessments at a national level (Footnote 1). I would like to encourage the citizens of these countries to look at their national assessments and, similar to the examples I have given in the case of Macedonia, begin creative dialogues within their own communities.

I urge my colleagues worldwide, change agents, coaches, leaders, to continue asking key important questions like:

How are we transforming conventional leaders into co-creative systemic leaders?
How are we shifting from EGO to ECO leadership?
What is the purpose of being, for the current generation of inhabitants on our planet Earth?
How will the planet look when we achieve the balance of body, emotions, mind, and spirit?

PLEASE BE CREATIVE IN FORMING LOCAL AND GLOBAL KEY QUESTIONS!

3. Presence – "The key to conscious and authentic leadership"

The success of particular intervention depends on the inner conditions of the intervener.

William O'Brien[45]

The observation of people and teams that are experiencing a state of flow leads to the conclusion that the quality and results produced by a team depend on the quality of presence of the members of that team. Above all, this depends on the presence of the leader and/or the leadership team.

QUALITY OF PRESENCE = QUALITY OF SYSTEM

As with most intangible, invisible or abstract things, **presence** is not a simple concept to describe. I'd even say that too many descriptions and words sometimes have the opposite effect when it comes to understanding what presence is.

To start describing presence, let me share what I recently heard in a lecture about presence by a masterful and very present teacher:

"The presence occurs only in the present moment."

Jeanne Hay
Teacher at the Ridhwan school[46]

Jeanne says that presence is not a thought, rather it is a being. Presence moves us towards greater internal depth, freedom and wisdom, and it is a **natural optimizing movement.**

My experience of presence is that it is a direct contact with our true nature (the true Self), a balanced state between relaxation and awareness in the present moment, and is the most natural state of our existence.

---

[45] Former CEO Hanover Insurance Com
[46] **Jeanne Hay** - http://www.ridhwan.org/school/

The four co-authors of the book "Presence", and global leaders in the areas of organizational leadership and social transformation, Peter Senge, Otto Scharmer, Joseph Javorski, and Betty Sue, when speaking of presence in the context of personal and organizational transformation, say that in order to be "born" in the new more complete world (in other words to break through and transform), we need to be open and **present**. They say that **without presence, we may have a superficial understanding, but no internal knowledge.**

Experiences show that presence is necessary to transport us from our comfort zone (the known) through the space of the unknown, to the territory of new knowledge and a creative existence. Because of this, **presence is one of the key qualities and skills necessary for new leaders, in the post conventional leadership paradigm. It is the essence of authentic transformation, in people and systems. Authentic leadership and presence go hand in hand.**

This has been noticed by Timothy Galway, one of the pioneers of modern coaching, who has described this in his book "The inner game"[47].
Galway emphasizes that the greatest enemy of man and his performance is his restless and self-critical mind, which Galway names **Self 1**.
Opposite to **Self 1** is **Self 2**, who is calm, present, and represents our natural potential and nested wisdom, who simply **"knows"**, just because this self exists in the moment – now.
To engage our natural potential, it is necessary to reduce the harmful effects of **Self 1** and to provide the natural existence of **Self 2**. This is best achieved when we remain present.

In the context of creative dialogue, as I mentioned previously, without a sufficient level of presence, teams/systems will continue to operate in the downloading zone of existence. Their containers are not tight enough, and they are vulnerable to the pressure of the creative tensions.
Without presence at the personal and team level, people are susceptible to their unconscious and paralyzing fears and limiting beliefs, and they are impulsive and reactive. They end up doing what they know, and performing in the comfort zone.

On an individual level, the leader who is not present could be considered as an "ego leader". S/he is not fully authentic, since s/he is not in touch with her/his

---

[47] Gallwey, W. Timothy (2000). *The inner game of work.* New York: Random House

true nature, and her/his motivations and actions stem from the ego structure, and/or the fears from the first three levels described by Barrett's model. Systems/communities led by ego leaders operate in an unbalanced and unstable way. This is obvious in the case of corporation Macedonia, but is also present all over the world.

This leader or the leadership team (and the system they lead) simply don't have a sufficient energetic capacity to inspire and lead the whole system in the zone of flow and balance. The Ego never has and never will have that capacity. The system remains fragmented and is not wholly unified.

With the increase of presence and the ability to hold the creative tension for longer intervals, there is a rise in the overall capacity for conscious awareness in the system, which helps the system to both relax and stay present in the natural "**NOW-ness**". These conditions within the container enable the system to collectively break through (penetrate, or rather dissolve) the walls of the comfort zone, and enter the zone of flow. Here the system touches the core of existence – our true nature, and its dynamic and inexhaustible reservoirs of wisdom, knowledge and creativity.

This is the place from which leaders, organizations, and humanity as a whole need to function in the 21st century. This is the presence zone, the zone of diamond leadership.

Naturally optimizing movement

When the presence is in the group, or the system is present, this can be felt, and it is not an unimaginable feeling or concept. The presence in the system has a density that is palpable, and when you feel it you will know without a doubt that you are in it, that you are present at a personal level and as a collective at the same time.

Presence is not material thing that you can buy, and the only way to learn and stay present is to practice being present.

One of the simplest and easiest ways of practicing presence (ideal for beginners who do not have much previous practice) is called the exercise of sensing[48].

The exercise of sensing:

You can practice this exercise on your own or in a group.

Just sit on a chair in a quiet room where you will not be interrupted.
Come to the front of the chair, without leaning your back against it. Straighten your spine. Place both your feet relaxed on the floor, and place the palms of your hands on your knees.
Close your eyes, and begin to pay attention to the sensations in your body.
Start to slowly circulate your attention, from the fingers on your right foot, towards the heel of the right foot, moving slowly towards the right knee, the thigh, the right part of your pelvis, and the sitting bone as it touches the chair. Move your attention slowly and carefully to the right side of your back, towards the right shoulder, the muscles of the arm, the right elbow, the forearm, the right wrist, and to the palm and fingers of your right hand.
Transfer your attention to the left hand, sensing the body in the same way – towards the left wrist, the forearm, the left elbow, towards the left shoulder, then down the left side of your back, towards the left pelvis, and the sitting bone. Slowly sense the left thigh, the knee, the left ankle, and the heel, becoming aware of your left foot and the toes at the end.
If your attention falls at any time during this sensing exercise, be persistent, and continue from where you lost the attention and sensations.
Do not push or put pressure on yourself for not practicing well or for losing attention. This is not an easy practice, although it sounds very simple. Mastering it takes years of committed practice. Just keep your intention of sensing the body and staying present.

If you are a beginner, I recommend that you find a partner or a group that will support you during such an exercise. Start with 5-10 minutes and gradually, when you feel ready, increase it to 15-20 minutes a day.

In case you run a creative dialogue, if you notice that the system is unstable, that people are downloading, or monologues dominate, stop the talk and ask the

---

[48] The practice of sensing is not the same as meditation. They are very similar, and have similar benefits for practicioners.
I recommend the sensing practice every time you decide to work with a creative dialogue.

participants to do a sitting practice. This will center you all, and put you in a better condition to continue.

Conclusion

Corporation Macedonia, like so many other organizations and nations on the planet, and indeed like the whole of humanity, is at a great historical and evolutionary crossroads.
The old ways and methods of functioning are not sufficient to lead us through the challenges in the time ahead of us. Technology on its own cannot save humanity from the mess we are in.
If the citizens and organizations in corporation Macedonia, and in the world as a whole, do not change their limiting Ego-based values and behaviors – and if our leaders do not transform their old ways of governance, and start to develop and use co-creative Eco platforms for the transformation of the system – we will hardly be able to move in the direction of creative, innovative, and sustainable ways of functioning and living.
With immediacy, we need to start to **co-create** our new desired future.
This requires genuine and present leadership, along with respect and a sincere desire for the true values and long-term strategy, and the **commitment of all citizens in the system, without exception.**

The answers to the essential questions of:

Who are you, and what are you as a person?
Who and what are we as a nation?
How do we want to live, and which leaders do we want to lead us?

Are answers that can only arise from us as a **whole**.

To answer them, and to lead the quality of life that we desire, it is only **WE** who are responsible and who decide. It is time to accept full and whole responsibility for our future.

The choice is ours.

www.ingramcontent.com/pod-product-compliance
Lightning Source LLC
Chambersburg PA
CBHW071518220526
45472CB00003B/1063